Simple Sermons on Evangelistic Themes

Simple Sermons on Evangelistic Themes

W. Herschel Ford

BAKER BOOK HOUSE
Grand Rapids, Michigan 49506

Copyright 1970 by Zondervan Publishing House
Grand Rapids, Michigan

Reprinted 1986 by Baker Book House
Grand Rapids, Michigan
with the permission of the copyright holder

Library of Congress Catalog Card Number: 73-146569
ISBN: 0-8010-3525-2

Third printing, January 1988

Printed in the United States of America

This book is lovingly dedicated to
Wanda and Fred Hooper
of Miami Beach, sweet and wonderful
friends who have meant so much to me.

CONTENTS

FOREWORD

This is my thirty-second volume of "Simple Sermons." I am deeply grateful to God for permitting me to write all of these books, and I am grateful to all those preachers and Christian workers who have told me that they have received a blessing from these messages.

The sermons in this volume have been preached in many revivals in many states. God has seen fit to bless their delivery. Now I do not know where I received the ideas and illustrations in these sermons. They have come from many sources, many servants of God. So I must acknowledge my debt to all whose ideas may be incorporated in these messages and my prayer is that God will use our combined efforts to bring glory to Him and souls to the Saviour.

Let me say what I have said in many of these books. Preachers and Christian workers are invited to use these messages as their very own.

W. Herschel Ford

1

GOD'S RECIPE FOR A REVIVAL
II Chronicles 7:14

It seems that nearly every Bible-believing religious leader is saying today that what we need now in America more than anything else is a revival of the old-time religion. Our pastors say it. They think of all the members whose names are on their church rolls and remember how unfaithful many of them are. They think of those who live for the world only and of some who are living in sin. And often there arises from their hearts the cry, "Oh, God, send a real revival to my church." And then we hear Billy Graham thundering out over the radio, saying, "The only thing that can save America is a revival of religion, a turning back to God." And our editors get into the act when they say, "We must return to the spiritual verities that made our nation great." They are simply saying that we need a revival of the old-time religion.

Now what is a revival? I give you my definition. A revival is an awakening of God's people, which causes them to become active for God. That meaning is wrapped up in the word itself. *Vive* means life and *re* means again. So the implication here is that the life is already there, the life of Christ in the individual Christian. But that life is still and dormant and needs to be stirred up, that it might engage in an activity for Christ for which the Christian was formed.

But someone will say, "I thought we had revivals so that men and women and boys and girls around us might be saved." That is true, for that is the end result of revival. But if the other takes place, if Christians wake up and live and serve and witness as they should, we would not have to worry about people being saved. They would see such a difference in the lives of Christians that they would say, "I need that which you have; tell me how I can get it."

God has a recipe for revival and it's found in an old book of the Bible. He says, "If my people, which are called by my name, shall humble themselves, and pray, and seek my face, and turn from their wicked ways; then will I hear from heaven, and will forgive their sin, and will heal their land." Let us look at this great text.

I. The Text Is Directed to God's People

"If my people, which are called by my name." That's where revival must start, in the hearts of His people. I would like to ask you if you are one of His people. Are you a real Christian or do you just bear the name? Are you a child of God or just a church member? Have you been redeemed or were you just baptized by some preacher? Jesus said, "Ye must be born again." Have you had that tremendous experience?

John 1:12 says, "As many as received him, to them gave he power to become the sons of God." Have you received Him into your heart and life? Acts 20:21 says it must be "repentance toward God, and faith toward our Lord Jesus Christ." Have you genuinely repented of your sin and put your faith in Him? Ephesians 2:8, 9 says, "By grace are ye saved through faith; and that not of yourselves: it is the gift of God: Not of works, lest any man should boast." Are you trusting fully in Him or are you depending upon your own works, your life, your character, your gifts? Are you really a child of God?

We are all saved by faith in Christ, although under different circumstances. When Paul was saved he was thrown to the ground, a bright light shone down upon him, and he was blinded for several days. But when Lydia was saved she was at a riverside prayer meeting where Paul spoke, and she was born again as quietly as a new day is born. Have you had this experience? Then this text is for you. If you haven't been born again, you can have that experience today.

II. THE TEXT TELLS US TO HUMBLE OURSELVES AND PRAY AND SEEK GOD'S FACE

This simply means that we are to go down on our faces before God. We are to acknowledge our sins, confess our shortcomings, and put aside everything that stands between us and God. But how much does the average Christian pray? He prays only when trouble arises. When his health is good, when his family is well, when the money is coming in, he forgets God and tries to squeeze all the happiness he can out of life. Then when he gets into a hole, when hard times come, he calls upon God.

But there are three kinds of prayer that ought to arise daily from our hearts. First, there is the prayer of gratitude, thanking God for all His blessings. Then there is the prayer for forgiveness, asking God to forgive us for our sins and to cleanse us from all unrighteousness. Then there is the prayer about service, asking God to fit us for service and to fill us with the Holy Spirit.

Dr. Chester Swor is a little, crippled layman who goes up and down the land, telling people about Jesus. When he graduated from college he secured a position on the faculty of a southern school. He said he had so many things to do that he didn't have time to get alone with God in prayer and Bible study. He felt himself slipping away from God and he didn't want this to happen. So he decided to arise an hour earlier each morning and spend that hour with God. He has kept up that custom over the years and has become one of the greatest Christians and most effective speakers for Christ in America. Yes, prayer changes things and prayer changes people. We are to humble ourselves, pray and seek God's face.

III. The Text Then Tells Us to Turn From Our Wicked Ways

Now, here's where the rub comes in; here is the reason we are not the Christians we ought to be. There is wickedness in us, there is sin in us, there are certain things standing between us and God. The psalmist told God to try him and see if there was any wicked way in him. Oh, we need to look deep down into our own hearts and lives and acknowledge the sin that is there. Not one of us is what we ought to be, we are guilty before God, we need to turn away from our wicked ways. Let us think of some practical ways in which we can do this.

1. *We need to turn away from our neglect of God's Word.* David says, "Thy word have I hid in mine heart, that I might not sin against thee" (Ps. 119:11). Is the Word of God hidden in your heart or merely between the covers of an old black Book which you seldom read?

The Bible is different from every other book. You read another book and you literally live for several days with the characters in the book. Then you finish the book and soon forget the names of the characters and the thread of the story. But it's different when you read the Bible. When you get into it, the Bible gets into you and changes your life.

One of my men told me on a New Year's Day that he was going to read the Bible through that year, so many chapters daily in the Old Testament and so many in the New. As he did this I saw him grow in grace and knowledge of the Saviour. Soon he was attending every service of the church, then soon he was tithing. Before long he was teaching a class of boys in the Sunday school and going out to witness for the Lord. He got in the Bible and let the Bible get in him and it changed his life.

There are three things we ought to do about the Bible. First, we should love it because it is God's love letter to us. Second, we should learn it and that requires study. Third, we should live it and that's the most important part of all.

2. *We need to turn away from our desecration of the Lord's Day.* The first day in the week is called a "holy day," but we have made of it a holiday. The largest crowds that gather for the sporting and entertainment events are the Sunday crowds.

Some years ago a fine young couple sat right in front of me at every church service. They would sit there with the love light shining in their eyes. I knew that they were in love. One day they came to see me and said, "We want to talk to you." I didn't ask them what they wanted. I just asked them when they wanted it, for I knew they wanted to be married. So one Saturday night I performed their marriage ceremony in a beautiful little wedding, and they went out to live happily in their apartment.

But soon I began to miss them from the church services from time to time. And it wasn't long until they were not there at all. Then one Sunday afternoon I rode down a highway which skirted a lake. One arm of the lake came right up to the highway. I looked down and saw my young couple down there in a new boat. I stopped the car and went down to talk to them. They gave me the old excuse about having to work hard during the week, so they came out on Sunday, to swim and boat and fish. I talked to them as a pastor should and they promised to come back to church.

But they did not come back. Then one day this young woman phoned me. She was weeping as she said to me, "Can you come over tonight and talk to us? Our marriage is about to go on the rocks." I went over that night and I advised them, I counseled with them, I prayed with them. But in a short time I read that they had been divorced. My fine young couple, so much in love at one time, were now estranged. And I truly believe that the marriage began to break up when they stopped coming to church. Something goes out of your life when you turn your back upon God and begin to desecrate His day.

Let me talk to you on Sunday night at eleven o'clock. As you tell me where you've been and what you have done that day, I can tell whether your life is counting for God or for the world.

3. *We need to turn away from a Christless home life.* America was founded upon Christian homes. Our forefathers had time to pray with their families, to read the Bible and talk about the things of God. But there are few homes like that today.

One of our missionaries had been out of the country for twenty-five years. He returned and went up and down the land, preaching in many churches and staying in many homes. Someone asked him what was the greatest change he had seen in American life. He did not speak of the jet planes, the color televisions, and other things. He said, "Before I went away I found a family altar in nearly every Christian home, now I seldom find one." There is the answer right there to the question of the breakdown in our home life.

Bobby Burns tells us of a good home in "The Cotter's Saturday Night." The humble laboring man, the father, would come home on Saturday night to be welcomed by his little family. After the evening meal was finished and the dishes washed and put away, the whole family would gather around the old organ and sing the songs of Zion. Then the father would reach up and take down the family Bible and slowly read a chapter from God's Word. Then he would fall on his knees and ask God to bless his humble home and family. And the poet goes on to say that "from scenes like these old Scotia's grandeur springs, that makes her loved at home, revered abroad."

Oh, that we might turn away from a Christless home life and give the Lord a place where He is loved and honored and spoken of!

4. *We need to turn away from a wrong attitude toward others.* Is there anything in your heart between you and someone else? Is there someone to whom you do not speak? Do you have hatred and envy and malice toward anyone? Then there is sin in your heart, a sin that displeases God and that will bring you unhappiness and eat away your spiritual joy and power.

Some years ago I was conducting a revival in a small Southern town. At every service, on the right side of the church auditorium, sat a young man, on the left side sat his father-in-law. These two men had not spoken to each other for twelve long years. They saw each other at church, they met each other on the street or at the post office. But, with hatred toward each other in their hearts, they never spoke. One day, at a day service, I preached on "Breaking the Alabaster Box." I pled with the people to get right with each other. When I gave the invitation and the congregation stood up to sing, I saw the son-in-law stand on tiptoe and look over toward his father-in-law. At the same time the older man looked over toward his son-in-law.

Then, as if a button had been pressed, the young man started toward the front from his side of the church and the older man started down from his side. The two men met in front of the pulpit and were about to shake hands with each other. But instead these two big men threw their arms around each other and wept and laughed and made up their differences. I want to tell you that a great revival broke out in that church and many souls were saved.

I do not know, but it may be that your wrong attitude toward someone else may keep back a revival from your church. I do know that your wrong attitude will hold back the blessings from your own heart and life. A real Christian can never be happy with an unchristian spirit in his heart.

5. *We need to turn away from our indifference to lost souls.* There are lost souls all around you. They may be in the place where you work, they may be a part of your social circle, they may be even in your own home. Do you care that they are lost? Do you have any concern for them? You

go into the state prison and the warden takes you down death row. He points to a certain cell and tells you that the man in that cell is to die in a few days in the electric chair. You look at the man. He is young and strong and vigorous, but in a few days his life will be snuffed out. He is a condemned man and you shudder as you think of what is going to happen to him. But there is something worse. John 3:18 tells us that a man without Christ is already condemned, not to die in the electric chair, but condemned to an eternal death in hell. How can we be indifferent to such a condition?

Dr. John A. Broadus was a great preacher and teacher of another day. He was reared in a country community in Virginia. One night in a revival service he went forward and gave his heart to the Saviour. Then he went back to his friend, Jim, and said, "Jim, won't you come and give your heart to Jesus? It's so wonderful." But Jim said, "Not tonight, John, but thank you for asking me." The next night Jim went forward and gave his heart to Jesus. When John went up to shake hands with him, Jim said, "Thank you for what you said to me last night, John, I never will forget it."

When John grew up he went away to become a great preacher, while Jim stayed in the community and became a farmer. Once every year John came back and preached one sermon in the country church. At the close of the service Jim would come up and give John a "pump-handle" handshake and say, "Thank you for what you said to me that night, John, I never will forget it." Some years later, when Dr. Broadus lay on his death-bed he said, "I know I am soon going out to heaven. First, I want to see Jesus and thank Him for saving me, then I want to find my old friend, Jim, and hear him say once more, 'Thank you for what you said to me that night, John, I never will forget it.'"

Oh, I wonder if anyone will ever meet you on the streets of glory and thank you for telling them about Christ and His saving grace. The poet said that "heaven would be two heavens in Immanuel's land if one soul from down here would meet you at God's right hand," one soul that you had won to Christ.

6. *We need to turn away from all sin and worldliness.* "Oh," you say, "I am all right, I am a member of the church, I have a good name in the community, there's nothing wrong with me." But God says, "All have sinned, and come short of the glory of God" (Rom. 3:23). And again, "If we say that we have no sin, we deceive ourselves, and the truth is not in us" (I John 1:8).

The trouble with us today is that we have the wrong conception of sin. We live in an age when "anything goes." We think if we haven't stolen or murdered anyone or if we haven't been drunk or committed adultery, that we have not sinned. We may have changed our ideas about sin, but God has not changed. He says, "The wages of sin is death" (Rom. 6:23). "Sin, when it is finished, bringeth forth death" (Jas. 1:15). Surely if we had the right conception of sin we would have more old-time genuine conviction for sin. Men would not say, "I want to join the church because my wife and children are members," or "I want to join because it will help my business or my standing in the community." No, they would come, crying out, "God be merciful to me, a sinner. What must I do to be saved?"

Yes, this is God's recipe for a revival. If all of God's people will get right with God, if they will go out to live rightly before Him, if they will witness faithfully for Him, God will keep His promise. He will send us a real revival.

Some years ago I had a preacher friend in Florida by the name of Dr. R. W. Hubert. He said that when he was a young man he held a meeting in a fine country church, and stayed in the nice home of the chairman of the board of deacons. He preached twice a day on Sunday, Monday, Tuesday and Wednesday, but nothing happened. There was not a move on the part of anyone. Then on Thursday morning he sat on the front porch, getting ready for the morning service. The deacon's daughter came out and said, "Brother Hubert, we are having a great meeting." He said, "Why do you say that?" She answered, "Because of what it has done for my father, the chairman of the board of deacons." "Tell me about it," he said.

"I have a younger sister named Emily," the young woman said. "A year ago she graduated from high school and father wanted her to go to college. But she was in love with a grocery clerk in a town twenty miles away and they wanted to get married. But father put his foot down and said, 'You're not going to marry anyone now; you are going to college.' But you know how young people are when they are in love, so one Sunday afternoon Emily and John went over to the county seat and were married. When they came back home father was furious. He said, 'Emily, take your clothes and leave. I don't want to see you again.' Now for the past year Emily has not been allowed to come home and mother and I never get to see her. She and John live in that town twenty miles away."

"But," she continued, "something has happened to father. Last Sunday when you preached your first sermon, he asked the pastor if he had told the visiting preacher anything about him. When the pastor said that he had not told you anything, father said, 'But he hit me right between the eyes this morning.' Just after breakfast this morning father said to mother, 'Mother, call Emily and tell her and John to come over and spend the day with us Sunday, and eat dinner with us and go to our meeting.' But mother said, 'No, dad, you are the one who drove her away. You'll have to be the one who invites her back.' So father called Emily and said, 'Emily, this is your father, we're having a good meeting at the church. We want you and John to come over Sunday and spend the day with us, eat dinner with us and go to church.' And Emily said that they would come."

On Sunday the church was filled with people when the service began, and the deacon sat in the "amen" corner. He kept looking at the door to see John and Emily come in. Finally they came in and started down the aisle. The deacon forgot all of his dignity; he ran down the aisle and met them. He threw one big arm around Emily and one big arm around John. And there before all the congregation they wept and laughed and made up their differences. Dr. Hubert said that he didn't preach a sermon that morning. He just gave a gospel invitation and thirty-five people came forward to give their hearts to Jesus. One of them was the deacon's son, who had stayed out of the church because of his father's bitter attitude.

One man got right with God and a revival came. Surely, if every member of your church would get right with God and go out to live and witness for Him, we would have a real revival. Don't you want that?

2

SALVATION BY GRACE

Ephesians 2:8-10

Some years ago I knew a little boy who lived in a small southern town. His family was very poor. His mother had died when he was four years of age. His father had married again and both his father and step-mother were very strict with the little boy. He did not get to go out and play as other boys did. There was always some work for him to do. He hardly ever went to church, because the other members of the family never went. Once in a while, when he had some new clothes, he would ask his father on Sunday morning for permission to go to Sunday school. Can you imagine a boy having to do that today?

Then two good men came to that town. A preacher and a singer came to conduct a revival meeting. Every night the little boy went to the meeting and sat up in one corner of the balcony. He heard the sweet singing and the good preaching and he saw boys and girls, men and women, go forward to give their hearts to Christ the Saviour. He wanted to do the same thing for his heart was broken because of his·lost condition. He wanted to become a Christian. But someone had given him the erroneous idea that if someone gave their hearts to Jesus and joined the church, they would have to give some money each Sunday, and he knew he couldn't do that. So every night, when the meetings were over, he would go by the cemetery where his mother was buried, go home and go to bed, where he would weep himself to sleep.

Several years later he moved to the big city and went to work. Then Billy Sunday came to the city for a revival campaign. The little boy went out to hear the great evangelist several nights. Then on Sunday afternoon Billy Sunday preached to men and boys only and this boy was there. At the close of the sermon Billy Sunday gave an invitation and pled for these men and boys to come to Christ. He called it "hitting the sawdust trail," for the meeting was held in a big tabernacle where sawdust covered the ground. Billy Sunday had been a big league baseball player and was very athletic, so he jumped down off the platform and stood there waiting to greet those who came forward. And this boy, moved by the Spirit of God, walked down the aisle to give his heart to Jesus. He put his hand in the great evangelist's hand, but he did more than that, he put his hand in the nail-pierced hands of Jesus. And after that everything was changed for that boy, for life was altogether different.

I know this is a true story for I was that boy. I don't remember Billy Sunday's sermon, I don't remember the songs that Homer Rodeheaver sang, I only know that the best I knew how, I gave my heart to Jesus that day. That has been a long time ago, but when I remember how Jesus saved me and called me to preach and how He has blessed me over the years, I say that my life has been a miracle of the grace of God. I can say with the Apostle Paul that "I am what I am by the grace of God."

Some years ago I went up to Billy's Island in the heart of the Okefenokee Swamp in South Georgia to preach over the weekend. I stayed in the home of the young man who was manager of the company commissary. He told me of the good things that had happened to him in his business and in his home. When I congratulated him, each time he would say, "All to Him I owe." As I look back over my life I can say the same thing, can't you?

Sam Jones, the great Methodist evangelist, had been a drunkard before he was converted. It is said that one day he stood on the sidewalk, talking to a friend. They saw a drunk man come reeling and staggering down the street and Mr. Jones said to his friend, "There, but for the grace of God, go I." And I wonder where you and I would be and where we would be headed if it were not for the grace of God. So let us look at this great text on grace.

I. The Text Tells Us That Some Are Saved and Some Are Lost

We find that truth all the way through the Word of God. "For God so loved the world, that he gave his only begotten Son, that whosoever believeth in him should not perish, but have everlasting life" (John 3:16).

"He that believeth on the Son hath everlasting life: and he that believeth not the Son shall not see life; but the wrath of God abideth on him" (John 3:36).

"He that believeth on him is not condemned: but he that believeth not is condemned already, because he hath not believed in the name of the only begotten Son of God" (John 3:18).

In each text we see that God has drawn a line right down the middle. On the one side we see those who are saved and have eternal life, on the other side there are those who are lost and shall not see life. Some years ago in one of our southern states a man and his wife had brutally murdered another man. They were sentenced to die on the gallows and every day, as they languished in their prison cell, they could hear the carpenters building the gallows. The buzz of the saw and the ring of the hammer brought to them anew the fact that they were condemned. But there is something worse, the man without Christ is condemned, not to die on the gallows, but to die eternally in hell.

There is no neutral ground. There are only two classes of people in the world, those who are saved and those who are lost, those who have trusted Christ and those who have rejected Him, those who are on the road to heaven and those who are on the road to hell.

After Adam's sin God came down to walk with him in the Garden of Eden, as He did each day at eventide. But Adam had hidden himself, so we hear God as He asks the first question in the Bible, "Adam, where art thou?" (Gen. 3:9). And I would like to ask you the same question. Where are you? Where do you stand? Are you for Christ or against Him? If you are not safe for heaven, I plead with you to come to Christ in this hour.

II.   The Text Tells Us That We Are Saved by Grace

Now what is grace? Certainly there is no more beautiful word in our language. We like to sing of "Amazing Grace" and the "marvelous grace of our loving Lord." But what does it mean? Someone said that grace was "the unmerited favor of a loving God." Someone else said that grace was "God's doing something for you that you couldn't do for yourself." Still another said that grace is "God's love outloving itself."

A Scottish preacher says that grace is "something that you need but do not deserve." I would like to go further than that and say that "grace is something you need but do not deserve, but which God gives you freely."

Now there are different kinds of grace. There is comforting grace. God has been called "the God of all comfort" (II Cor. 1:3). In time of sorrow no one can comfort as He can. Let's try our definition. Comforting grace is something you need but don't deserve, but which God gives you freely.

There is living grace. Paul said, "I can do all things through Christ which strengtheneth me" (Phil. 4:13). We need strength to enable us to live every day. Strength to live, living grace, is something we need but don't deserve, but which God gives us freely.

There is provisional grace. Paul said, "My God shall supply all your need according to his riches in glory by Christ Jesus" (Phil. 4:19). We need for God to provide for us every day. Provisional grace is something we need but do not deserve, but which God gives us freely.

Then there is dying grace. Paul had that and he came down to death with triumph in his heart and hope in his soul. When we come to the end of the way we'll want to feel God's presence with us. Dying grace is something we'll need. We won't deserve it, but God will give it to us freely.

But the reference in the text is to saving grace. "By grace are ye saved." Above all things we need salvation, but not one of us deserves it. We have sinned against God, we have broken His commandments, we deserve only to die eternally. But God freely gives us saving grace.

A Chinese gentleman was gloriously saved. In speaking of it later he said, "I knocked at the door of Buddha and found that he was dead, he could not help me. I knocked at the door of Confucius and there was no answer. I knocked at the door of Mohammed and there was nothing but an empty ring. But when I knocked at the door of Jesus, He opened the door and invited me in. He took away my sins, received me into God's family and put a new song in my heart." Now that is grace, saving grace. That's what Jesus will do for all who come to Him.

III. The Text Tells How We Can Appropriate That Grace

"By grace are ye saved through faith." It is God's grace and our faith which bring salvation. Grace is like a reservoir of cold water on a hot day, and faith is the cup that we use to bring the cooling drink to our lips. Grace is the remedy for our sin and faith is taking the medicine. Grace is the gift of heaven and eternal life and faith is our hand reaching up for it.

Now faith plays a big part in our daily lives. We eat at a restaurant and have faith that the cook did not poison the food. We work for a firm for a month and have faith that they will pay us for our services at the end of the month. We board a plane and have faith that we will be carried safely to our destination. (Of course, I always breathe a prayer when we take off, but that's faith, also.) We lend a man ten dollars and have faith that he'll pay us back on payday. We often misplace our faith and suffer for it. But when we put our faith in Jesus Christ we are saved and safe forever.

True faith consists of two elements, belief and trust. Just suppose that I had a thousand dollars in my pocket. I go down to the big National Bank and I ask the president, "Can you keep my money safely for me?" When he assures me that they can, I say, "Prove it to me." So he shows me the big steel vaults with their great doors, he shows me the various safety devices they have, he points out the employees of honesty and integrity. Then he shows by the bank's record that no one has ever lost a penny left in their care. Then I say, "I believe it; I believe you can keep my money safely." But if I go out of the bank with the thousand dollars still in my pocket, I have not exercised faith. I have believed but I have not trusted. If I had turned over my money to them I would have been exercising faith.

Some men say, "I believe all you say about Christ. I believe He was born of a virgin, that He lived a sinless life, that He died on the cross, that He rose from the dead and will return to earth someday." But that is not enough to save anyone. "The devils believe and tremble." In order to exercise faith one must not only believe all these things about Christ, he must trust Him with all he has for time and eternity. He must come to Jesus with his poor, lost sinful soul and say, "Here, Lord, I give myself away, 'tis all that I can do."

Now, of course, repentance must be coupled with faith. Paul said it must be "repentance toward God, and faith toward our Lord Jesus Christ" (Acts 20:21). So I beg you to repent of your sin, and put your faith in Jesus Christ. Then you'll become a child of God and all the demons in hell will not be able to sever that relationship.

IV. The Text Tells Us That All of This Is Not of Ourselves

Our repentance, our faith and our salvation do not come from ourselves, but from God. "Salvation is of the Lord." When I was in the pastorate hardly a Sunday went by but that a Sunday school teacher or a mother or father would bring a little boy or girl by the church office to talk to me about being saved and joining the church. I would carefully explain the plan of salvation to them, then I always asked them this question, "Did you ever feel, when I gave the invitation, that you would like to come forward and confess Christ as your Saviour?" When they answered, "Yes," I would then ask, "Who put that feeling in your heart and mind?" And without exception they always said, "God" or "Jesus."

It is true. Our salvation does come from God. He is the One, through His Spirit, who convicts men of sin and points them to the Saviour. He causes men to repent; He causes them to have faith in His Son. We just let go and let God have His way and He does it all.

V. The Text Tells Us That Salvation Is the Gift of God

Yes, He gave us His Son, and when we trust Him He gives us eternal life. "The gift of God is eternal life through Jesus Christ our Lord" (Rom. 6:23).

A little boy, whose mother was dead, had a father who was a drunkard. One day the boy was in a tragic accident and lay critically ill in the hospital. His father, sober now, came to see him. The father said, "Son, you must get well now and daddy will quit drinking and be a good daddy to you." But the little fellow said, "No, dad, I'm not going to get well." "You must get well, son, and I'll look after you. I'll go to Sunday school and church with you. I'll be a good daddy, son." But the little boy said, "No, dad, I'm not going to get well, but when I'm gone I want you to remember that I loved you, even if you did get drunk." The little boy did die, but his dying testimony led his father to Christ.

That is a slight picture of God. We have sinned, we have broken His laws, we have trampled His Son under foot, we have turned our backs upon Him. But He still loves us. He says, "Even if you have sinned I love you and I have a gift for you. Here is eternal life and I will gladly give it to you."

But a gift is of no value unless you receive it. If I could give you a million dollars, it would not help you one bit unless you received it. And God's gift for you is of no value unless you receive it.

When Andrew Jackson was our president a man by the name of Wilson was sentenced to die for a crime he had committed. But the governor of the state issued him a pardon. He refused to accept the pardon. He said, "I don't want the pardon, I don't want to live, I want to die." They insisted that he take the pardon, he insisted that he didn't have to receive it. The case was taken all the way to the Supreme Court. The court decreed that Wilson did not have to accept the pardon. They said that a pardon was of no value unless a man was willing to receive it, so Wilson died. God in His mercy and grace, offers you a pardon. But you say, "I will not receive it." Then all that Christ did for you on Calvary is of no value to you, and you die eternally.

VI. The Text Tells Us That Salvation Is Not of Works, Lest Any Man Should Boast

We are so vain, that if works could save, we would boast all over heaven about what we did to get there. One man would say, "I built a hospital." Another would say, "I endowed a college." Another would say, "I preached for forty years." Another would say, "I was a deacon and a tither." But when we get to heaven we'll forget all that we have done and just brag on Jesus. The theme song in heaven is, "Worthy is the Lamb." If we were to go up there and sing about our works and our worthiness, an angel would throw us out of heaven.

Yes, salvation is all of grace, but there are some things that we are to do after we have been saved. That is why we must include verse 10 in this message. It says that we have been "created in Christ Jesus unto good works." Here is God's simple plan for us. We are saved by grace, then we are to engage in good works for Him. Now what will the truly redeemed person want to do after he has been saved?

1. *He will want to be obedient in baptism.* Baptism does not save anyone, but if you have been saved you will not let anything keep you back from the baptismal waters. You may never preach a sermon in some pulpit, but you preach a great pictorial sermon in baptism, a sermon with three points. First, baptism pictures the death, burial and resurrection of Christ. Second, it portrays what has happened to the true convert. He has died to the old life, the "old man" is buried and he is raised to walk in newness of life. Third, baptism gives us a prophetic picture. As we are raised from the liquid grave, we remember how we shall be raised when Jesus comes in the air.

2. *He will become a faithful church member.* His church will come before his club, his lodge, his social engagements. And he will keep his membership alive. He will not move to some other place and leave his church membership behind, just as a name on some church roll. For then he will soon drift away even from God Himself. Some people move away and let twenty-five or thirty years go by without joining a church in their new location. If I did that I would begin to doubt my salvation.

3. *He will live a consecrated Christian life.* There are two kinds of Christians in the world today. Some live for Christ, some live for the world. Some live to glorify Christ, some live only for self. Some have a mighty influence for the Lord, some have only a negative influence. Some will receive a reward for their faithfulness, some will find their works burned up at the end of the way.

One afternoon, when I was pastor in El Paso, I took my youth director, Earl McCuin, out to make some pastoral calls. We visited two men in their eighties that afternoon.

I asked the first man if he was a Christian and church member. He replied, "No, I joined a Baptist Church when I was twenty years of age, but I soon quit. I haven't been to church for over sixty years." I talked to him the best I could. Then I had a prayer for him. When I said "Amen" at the close of the prayer, he said, "So mote it be." Then I knew his trust was more in his lodge than in the Lord.

Then we went to see the other man. He said, "My life is draining out like water out of a sponge." He told me how he missed going to church and hearing his pastor's sermons. We talked for some time about God's goodness, then I said, "Let me have a prayer for you." He said, "Let me pray first." He prayed a very fervent prayer, then I offered a prayer. When we left his room I said to Earl, "That was a good prayer the old man offered, wasn't it?" And Earl said, "Yes, you could tell he had been there before."

Both of these men died in a few days, but what a difference. One man had wasted a whole lifetime and all he could hold to was a lodge motto at the end of the way. The other man, as he entered the gates of glory, could talk to God as a man talks to his best friend.

I call on you to live a consecrated Christian life. If you want the best in two worlds, live your life for Jesus.

4. *He will want to have a part in all of God's good work on this earth.* This means service to God and man. It means supporting His work with time, talent and the tithe. It means telling others at home and abroad about Jesus.

Now we go back to the meaning of grace. It is something we need, but do not deserve, but which God gives us freely. All that we have of life and health here is because of the grace of God. And all the hope we have for the future life is because of this same grace. This fact ought to make us want to live at our best for Him every day.

In the years gone by an old man in the southeastern part of our country contracted tuberculosis. He was sent to a small town in Arizona with the hope that the disease could be arrested. His faithful wife went along with him. But his condition became more critical every day. The pastor in the little town went to see him and they became good friends. Nearly every day the preacher visited the old man and they would talk and read the Bible and pray together, and sometimes even sing a hymn together.

Then early one morning the preacher felt a premonition that he ought to go over to see the old man before breakfast. The sun was just rising over the eastern horizon as he made his way to the little house. When he arrived and after the usual greetings had been exchanged, the old man said, "Preacher, I'm in such misery and pain here. Do you think it would be a sin if I asked God to let me die today?" The preacher looked up at the old man's wife and she said, "Of course I would miss him, but he suffers so much here, so I believe it would be best for him if he could go on and be with the Lord." They told the old man it would be all right, so he began to pray. "Lord," he prayed, "I'm in so much misery and pain here. I want to come and be with Thee. I haven't been able to do much for You here, but I want to come and lay my few sheaves at Thy golden feet." Then he prayed for his wife, the preacher and many others. Then he began to sing:

> Jesus, Lover of my soul,
> Let me to Thy bosom fly,
> While the nearer waters roll,
> While the tempest still is high.

And before the first stanza was ended his voice trailed away into silence and his soul went out to be with God. Just as the sun started its bright journey over the world, the old man's soul began a brighter journey to live a brighter life with Christ.

Oh, my friends, that hour is coming for you and me. It may be soon, it won't be long. Are you ready for that hour? Have you been saved by His grace? If not, I urge you to come to Jesus now.

3

YE MUST BE BORN AGAIN

John 3:3

One night when Jesus rested from the weary labors of the day a very prominent man came to see Him. The name of this man was Nicodemus. He was a man of position, of prominence, of power and probably of wealth. But this man was not satisfied with life. There was a great hunger in his heart. The things of earth did not satisfy. He was always reaching out for something that would bring him happiness, but joy and happiness and peace seemed always to elude him. Then he heard about Jesus, about His wonderful spirit, His marvelous attitude toward sinners, His great teachings and mighty works. So Nicodemus must have said, "If that Man ever comes my way, I will seek Him out and pour out my heart to Him. Maybe He can help me."

And in the due course of time Jesus did come to the city where Nicodemus lived. So, under the cover of darkness, Nicodemus slipped out to see Jesus and to bare his heart to Him. And Jesus looked into the soul of this hungry-hearted man and said, "Nicodemus, you must be born again. You have many things that the world can give you, but you'll never find peace and joy until you have been born again." He would say the same thing if He were here today. The world is full of men who are trying to find happiness in this world. They go everywhere and do everything to find some zest in life, but their search is in vain. Jesus would say to them today, "You're seeking for satisfaction in the wrong place. Come to Me and be born again and all the joys of earth and heaven will be yours."

Jesus said, "Except a man be born again, he cannot see the kingdom of God." Now you may see many wonderful things in this world. You may see the great redwood trees of California, some of them so large that a car can be driven through their trunks, but you'll never see the Tree of Life in heaven unless you have been born again. You may see the great rivers of the world as they make their way toward the sea, but you'll never see the River of Life that flows by the throne of God unless you have been born again. You may see the great cities of the world in all their glory, but you'll never see the Holy City of the New Jerusalem unless you have been born again. You may see the great countries of the world in all their splendor, but you'll never see the land that is fairer than day unless you've been born again. You may live in the finest houses that money can buy, but you'll never see the Father's house of many mansions unless you've been born again. You may receive degrees from the greatest colleges and universities, but you'll never see heaven unless you have God's B.A. degree, God's "born again" degree.

I. The Necessity of Regeneration

Jesus said, "Ye must be born again." He emphasized the "must." This is one of His divine imperatives. In order to get to heaven it isn't absolutely necessary that you be baptized, yet if you have really found Christ as your Saviour, nothing will keep you out of the baptismal waters. Still, it is not your baptism that saves you. In order to get to heaven, it isn't absolutely necessary for you to be a church member, but if you have been saved nothing can keep you out of a church. Yet, it isn't your church membership that saves you. In order to get to heaven it isn't absolutely necessary that you tithe, but if you really love Christ you will surely tithe.

Yet, it isn't your gifts that save you. Here it is, here is the one thing necessary, "Ye must be born again."

When I served as a pastor in El Paso, Texas, the federal judge invited me to come down to the Federal Courthouse and speak at a ceremony where 110 aliens were to be naturalized, that is, they were to become United States citizens. They were there from England, from Japan, from Germany, from Mexico and several other countries. They had been in the United States for some time and had decided that they wanted to become United States citizens. So the government prescribed certain procedures for them before they could become citizens. They had to study certain principles and truths and history. Then they had to pass certain examinations. Then they had to take certain vows and promise loyalty to the United States. When they had done all these things they became citizens of our great country.

In like manner, a sinner is not a citizen of heaven, he is a foreigner to the grace of God. If he wants to become a citizen of heaven and a child of God, he, too, must go through a certain process, something special must happen to him. And here it is, "Ye must be born again."

You look at a man who is living in sin and you say, "He'll never get to heaven, something must happen to him." You are simply saying, "He must be born again."

A man must be born again because of the difference in his nature and the nature of God. Man by nature is a sinner, he was born in sin, he lives in sin, he walks in sin. But God is sinless, perfect, spotless, altogether righteous. How can a sinful man ever go to heaven and walk the golden streets of glory? He can never do this until something happens to him. And here it is in Jesus' own words, "Ye must be born again."

II. THE NATURE OF REGENERATION

1. *It is not a reformation.* Someone says, "I am going to turn over a new leaf. I am going to give up some of the bad things I have been doing." That's reformation, but that's

not regeneration. God may not have been in this decision at all, it may have been something done for the benefit of the person making such a statement.

In the early days of my ministry I taught a Sunday school class of young men. One young fellow in the class was addicted to strong drink. He got off on a drunken spree and when he returned he was ill at home. I went to see him and he said, "I'm not going to drink anymore. The doctor told me if I kept on drinking, that some day I might go out like a light. So I am giving up drink." This was not regeneration. The young fellow didn't give a thought to God in his decision. He was reforming for his own good. It did not mean that he had been born again.

Regeneration brings reformation, but reformation is not regeneration. An evangelist in other days went up and down the land, preaching that people should "quit their meanness and join the church." Now many people have quit their meanness and have never joined a church, while many people have joined the church and have never quit their meanness. Reformation is not regeneration. If you could live from now until your dying day without committing a single sin, that would not blot out the old record of sin against you. You must be born again.

2. *It is not merely a profession of religion.* Some years ago I knew a certain man who lived wholly without God and made no claim to be a Christian. He never went to church, he had nothing to do with any of the things of God. One morning my doorbell rang and a neighbor came to say, "That man woke up this morning, said one word to his wife, then dropped back on his pillow in death." I was called on to conduct the funeral. In those days funerals were sometimes conducted in the home. As I started up the steps to conduct the service a man called me aside and asked me if I was the preacher who was to have the service. When I told him that I was, he said, "That man was my brother and I wanted you to know that twenty-five years ago he made a profession of religion in a lumber camp." I guess he expected me to go in and preach his brother right into the

gates of glory, but the dead man had lived a godless life all of his years. An empty profession of religion is not regeneration. Regeneration goes down deeper than the lips and changes the whole heart and life.

My men of the church often went out on Thursday nights to visit the unsaved men of the city. Often they would come back rejoicing and saying, "Pastor, Mr. So-and-So made a profession of faith in his home tonight." I would rejoice with them, but so many times we could not get those who had made a profession to come near the church or to make their profession public, or to come for baptism. They had made an empty profession with their lips which meant nothing. Such a profession is not regeneration.

3. *It is not merely spiritual culture.* Culture on the outside does not change character on the inside. You may have gone to church all of your life, you may have been surrounded with the best forms of spiritual culture, but that is not enough, that is not regeneration. A prominent preacher once said, "My two little girls do not need to be born again. They have lived in a spiritual atmosphere all of their lives. They have gone to Sunday school and church every Sunday, they have heard us ask the blessing at every meal, they have shared in the family altar where we prayed and read the Bible. They don't need regeneration." But he was wrong. Even in the nature of those dear little girls there was sin and, like everyone else, they did need to be born again.

When I was a boy I heard a preacher use this illustration. It may be a bit crude, but it illustrates my point. He said that you could bring a pig in out of the pigpen, give him a good bath, sprinkle him with expensive perfume, tie a red ribbon around his neck and put him in the living room. But he said that as soon as a back door would open, the pig would run out the door, find a mudhole and wallow in it, bath, perfume, red ribbon and all. That's the nature of a pig. You may surround him with all of these things externally but that doesn't change his nature, that doesn't change him on the inside. And you can surround a sinner with the finest type of spiritual culture, but that doesn't change his nature. He is still a sinner. He must be born again.

4. *It is not morality.* Nicodemus had to be a man of high morals to have the position he held, but Jesus said to him, "Ye must be born again." The rich young ruler declared that he had kept the moral law all of his life, but Jesus said to him, "One thing thou lackest." You may be the cleanest moral man in the world, but without the new birth you are eternally lost.

Morality and a good life are fine as far as they go, but they don't go far enough. I well remember the first time I saw the ocean. I traveled by train to Daytona Beach, Florida, to visit my only sister and her family and arrived there around midnight. Her house was just about a block from the ocean. I went to sleep that night with the sound of the surf singing in my ears. The next morning when I looked upon the ocean for the first time I felt like saying with Mark Twain, "It's a success." Well, there is a long fishing pier running out about 1,200 feet into the Atlantic Ocean. Many people go out there and fish off the end of the pier.

Just suppose that I were to say to you, "I'm going to get on this pier and walk to Europe." You would say, "Man, you're crazy." But I would say, "Just watch me." I would walk out about 400 feet on the pier and I would say, "You see, I'm all right, I'm perfectly dry, I'm walking to Europe." Then I would walk out another 400 feet and I would say, "I'm on my way, I'm walking to Europe." But if I walked out another 400 feet I would come to the end of the pier and my walk to Europe would be over. You see, it was good as far as it went, but it didn't go far enough.

It's the same way with our morality and good lives. They are fine as far as they go, but they don't go far enough. They'll never get you to heaven. You must be born again.

5. *It is not a matter of good works.* We do not work in order to be saved, we work because we have been saved. All of our good works, inside the church and out, can never save us. The Bible tells us that our righteousness is but as "filthy rags" and we can never approach God in such rags.

We need to be clothed in His righteousness, we must be born again.

Romans 6:23 says, "The gift of God is eternal life through Jesus Christ our Lord." It is not a matter of our works, it is a matter of God's gift which is ours the minute we are born again. Ephesians 2:8, 9 says, "For by grace are ye saved through faith; and that not of yourselves: it is the gift of God: Not of works, lest any man should boast."

Our works for God have nothing to do with our salvation, but they do determine our rewards in heaven. Let me illustrate. Suppose that I were a very wealthy man and that I owned a steamship as large and luxurious as the *Queen Mary* or the *U.S.S. United States*. (You'll have to stretch your imagination right here.) And suppose that I offered you a free trip to Europe on my ship. Then when we are a day or two out from New York I come to you and say, "I'm a little shorthanded in the purser's office. Can you help me out?" You would say, "Yes, I'll be glad to help you." Then when we reach Europe I would come around and hand you a check for $200.00. You would ask, "Why are you giving me this check?" and I would reply, "I am paying you for the work you did in the office on the way over." You would say, "I don't expect any pay. You gave me the trip and that's enough." Then I would say, "Yes, I promised you a free trip, but because you worked on the way over, this is an extra reward."

That is the way God does. He says, "I promised you a free trip to heaven if you would trust My Son as your Saviour, but because you worked for Me on the way to glory, I am going to give you an extra reward." So if you work for the Lord He'll reward you at the Judgment Seat of Christ, but your works do not save you. You must be born again.

6. *It is not baptism.* All the baptismal waters in the world cannot wash away a single sin. That sin must be washed away in the precious blood of the Lamb (I Peter 1:19). Baptism comes after salvation. It is a matter of obedience to Christ after one has been saved.

The minute a person is saved his first impulse is to follow

Christ in baptism. Nothing will keep him out of the baptismal waters. But baptism is not regeneration. You must be born again.

7. *It is not church membership.* Going into a church doesn't make you a Christian anymore than going into a garage makes you an automobile. The church is the home of the saved, it is not the Saviour. Now Jesus founded the church and put it down here for us to live in and serve through. If we are saying that we can live a good Christian life out of the church, if we say that we don't need the church, we are simply saying that Christ made a mistake when He put it down here, and that is our mistake.

I like to think of the church in this way. During World War II our great aircraft carriers were stationed in the South Pacific. The pilots on the carrier would load their planes with fuel and ammunition, then they would fly off the deck and go out to accomplish their mission. They would drop their bombs, complete their missions, then fly back to the carrier for a new supply of fuel and ammunition. The church is like that carrier. We come to church on Sunday morning and Sunday night and Wednesday night and we take on new spiritual strength and energy. Then we go out during the week to use that power for the Lord. We go out to live for Christ and witness for Him and accomplish the mission for which Christ leaves us in the world. Then we come back to church again to renew our strength and energy. But church membership is not regeneration. You must be born again.

8. *Positively regeneration is a change wrought in the heart and life by Almighty God.* It is a change that comes from above. "Salvation is of the Lord." Once I traveled down a tidal river to the place where it emptied into the Atlantic Ocean. Normally that river runs in a southeasterly direction, but twice each day, when the tide comes in, it turns around and flows in a northwestward direction. When the mighty horses of the sea come charging in, the river makes a complete about-face.

It's the same way in salvation. A man is headed toward

death and hell as he walks in sin. But when he is born again, when Christ comes in, he turns around and is soon walking toward life and heaven. And it is all the work of God through the Holy Spirit.

Can you stop the sun from shining or cause the storm to cease its roar? Can you change the Ethiopian's skin or the leopard's spots? Can you bore through a steel beam with a tallow candle? No, but you can do any of these things easier than you can save yourself. Regeneration is the work of the Lord in the human heart.

9. *Regeneration is a mysterious change.* "The wind bloweth where it listeth, and thou hearest the sound thereof, but canst not tell whence it cometh, and whither it goeth; so is every one that is born of the Spirit" (John 3:8). Now this is a mystery, but we ought to be willing to leave the mystery with God. We accept the many things in this world that we don't understand, why not accept spiritual truths that we cannot understand with these finite minds?

For instance, a black cow goes out into the pasture and eats green grass. She comes home at night and gives white milk. In a few days that white milk is churned and you get yellow butter. Now there it is. Black cow, green grass, white milk and yellow butter. You don't understand all the chemical and color changes, but tomorrow morning you'll spread that butter on your toast and drink the milk. You accept what you do not understand.

I have a color television set in my living room. I can sit across the room and watch a football game on the television screen, I can hear a speech being made a thousand miles away, I can see something happening and can hear the sounds of it from the other side of the world. But those sounds and those pictures come into my living room through a black wire no larger than my finger. I don't understand it, but I'm not going to throw my television set out of the window. We accept these things that we don't understand, why not accept the mysterious things of a great God?

One night you sat in a church. It may have been a small country church, it may have been a large city church. You heard the Gospel and you were deeply convicted for your sin. You could hardly sleep that night or eat the next day, so deep was your conviction. You came back to the church the next night and the conviction grew deeper. When the invitation was given you went forward and gave your heart to Christ. Something happened to you. The burden was lifted and you went out of the church with a song in your heart. And life has been different ever since. You didn't understand what had happened, but you thank God that it did happen. Regeneration is a mysterious change.

10. *Regeneration is an absolute change.* II Corinthians 5:17 says, "Therefore if any man be in Christ, he is a new creature: old things are passed away; behold, all things are become new." Oh, we've seen it so many times. We have seen a man deep in sin. Then we lost track of him. Several years later, when we saw him again, he was living a devoted and useful Christian life. He had been born again; he was a new creature in Christ Jesus.

A man was gloriously saved one night. The next morning he stood by the kitchen window, looking out as his wife prepared breakfast. He said, "Honey, I never saw the grass so green or the trees and flowers so beautiful." What had happened? The grass and flowers and trees had not changed, he had changed. He had been born again and all the world looked different. Regeneration is an absolute change.

III. What Does One Do to Secure the New Birth?

1. *He hears the Gospel.* "Faith cometh by hearing, and hearing by the word of God" (Rom. 10:17). "The gospel of Christ is the power of God unto salvation" (Rom. 1:16).

You have heard the Gospel today and maybe have heard it many times. You have heard it from eloquent lips and from dull but earnest lips. You have heard it from many pulpits. You have already met this first requirement.

2. *He is convicted for sin.* A man must know he is lost before he can be saved. On the day of Pentecost the crowd who heard Peter preach, convicted of their sin, cried out,

"Men and brethren, what shall we do?" (Acts 2:37). They were convicted of their sin. And the Philippian jailer said to Paul and Silas, "What must I do to be saved?" (Acts 16:30). He was convicted of his sin.

3. *He repents of his sin.* Repentance is a godly sorrow which causes a man to turn away from his sin and turn toward Christ. No one is ever saved unless he repents of all his sin.

4. *He trusts Christ as His Saviour.* He turns from sin in repentance and turns to Christ in simple, child-like faith. It is "repentance toward God and faith toward our Lord Jesus Christ" (Acts 20:21). The Bible says that "he that believeth on the Son hath everlasting life" (John 3:36).

The Bible says, "He that heareth my word, and believeth on him that sent me, hath everlasting life" (John 5:24). The Bible says, "Believe on the Lord Jesus Christ, and thou shalt be saved" (Acts 16:31). Then, after you have repented of your sin and put your trust in Christ, you will confess Him as your Saviour. "If thou shalt confess with thy mouth the Lord Jesus, and shalt believe in thine heart that God hath raised him from the dead, thou shalt be saved. For with the heart man believeth unto righteousness; and with the mouth confession is made unto salvation" (Rom. 10:9, 10).

Now this is for you. This is what you need most of all. You go to the funeral parlor and you look into the face of a young man who lies in his casket. He has two hands but he cannot use them. He has two feet but he cannot walk. He has two ears but he cannot hear. He has two eyes but he cannot see. He has a mouth but he cannot speak. What does he lack? He lacks one thing, he lacks the breath of life. You may have health and wealth, you may have prestige and position, you may have many things that life can give, but you are not a complete man. You lack one thing, without which life is empty and there is no hope of heaven. You must be born again.

In my first pastorate a certain man contracted tuberculosis. The doctors urged him to go to the sanitarium. They felt that they could arrest his case. But he refused to go.

He said, "I owe several more payments on my home. I'll work until I pay my home free of debt, then I'll go to the sanitarium." He could not be turned from his purpose, so he kept on working until he paid for his home, then he broke down and was carried to the sanitarium. I went out to see him one night and they told me he had died five minutes before my arrival. It was all right for him to work hard, it was all right for him to pay for his home, but in so doing he neglected the main thing, his health. It is all right for you to get an education, to buy your home, to provide for your family, but don't neglect the main thing, your salvation. You must be born again.

A preacher was called to visit a dying man in the hospital. He tried to talk to the man but the man was too far gone. He kept on saying, "Oh, Jesus, can't You help me?" And he died, whispering, "Oh, Jesus, can't You help me?"

Yes, Jesus can help you tonight. He can save you and put you on the road to heaven. What will you do with Him? Ye must be born again.

4

FIVE TREMENDOUS THOUGHTS FOR TIME AND ETERNITY

Romans 6:23

Some years ago a prominent preacher conducted a revival in a small west Texas town. One night he preached on "Time and Eternity," using five points in his message. That night a little boy, convicted of his sin, went forward and accepted Jesus Christ as his Lord and Saviour. That little boy later felt that God was calling him to be a gospel preacher, and now he is Dr. Jess C. Moody, illustrious pastor of the great First Baptist Church of West Palm Beach, Florida.

Now in this message I am going to use the same five points that the preacher used the night Jess was saved. This will be the simplest evangelistic sermon you have ever heard. Without any further introduction, let me give you the first point.

I. Life Is Short

The Bible says that life is like a vapor (James 4:14). I can remember when I was a boy, the wood-burning stove that sat in the corner of the kitchen. On that stove was an iron kettle and from the spout of that kettle the steam, the vapor would pour out. But I noticed that it disappeared before it reached two feet into the air. The Bible says life is like that, life is short.

Then the Bible says that life is like a weaver's shuttle (Job 7:6). Have you ever seen an old-fashioned loom. There is a handle on one side and a man pulls that handle, then the shuttle shoots back and forth across the loom, back and forth, back and forth, in a split second's time. The Bible says life is like that.

My mother prepared our breakfast for us one Friday morning when I was a small child, but she died that night at eight o'clock. Life is short. I visited one of my members in the hospital one Saturday afternoon. He was sitting up in a chair. He said, "I'm feeling fine and I'm going home tomorrow." But he died that night. Life is short. One of my deacons was at prayer meeting on Wednesday night. On Thursday morning someone called me to tell me that he had just died very suddenly. I rushed down to the house and arrived there before the undertaker. The man was sitting on the couch, the morning paper by his side, but he was dead. Life is short.

I held a meeting with a fine pastor in Anchorage, Alaska. He told me that he was going to Tacoma, Washington, for a meeting the next week. He seemed to be in perfect health but he died suddenly in Tacoma. Life is short. I was scheduled to conduct a revival in Warren, Arkansas, but a few weeks before the revival the splendid pastor dropped dead on the golf course and the meeting was cancelled. Life is short. I conducted a meeting in a small Texas town. A layman went out to talk to another man about his salvation. The layman made this notation on a card and dated it January 10th, "This man says that he does not need any change of heart and life." I have this card in my possession and on the bottom are these words, dated January 14th, "This man died this morning." Life is short.

We read about a person dying at 90 or 100 years of age and we say, "That's a long time to live." But Methuselah lived 969 years and even that is a short time compared to eternity. Suppose that your life was ending today, what would it be like? Would it be a time of sorrow or a time of joy? Would it be a time of regret or a time of hallelujah?

As Thomas Paine, the author and atheist, lay dying, he cried out, "I would give worlds if I hadn't written *The Age of Reason*. Oh, Lord, help me. Oh, Christ, help me. Stay with me, for God's sake. Send even a little child to stay with me for it is hell to be alone. If the devil ever had an agent, I am that one." I tell you, men ought not to die like that.

When Adoniram Judson, the missionary, was dying, he said, "I go with the gladness of a boy bounding away from school. I feel so strong in Christ." Catherine Booth, the Salvation Army worker, said, "The waters are rising, but so am I. I am not going under but over. Do not be concerned about dying. Go on living for Christ and dying will be all right." General Stonewall Jackson was accidentally fired upon by his own troops as he returned to camp one night. As he died a few days later he said, "I am just going to cross over the river and rest beneath the trees on the other side." And the Apostle Paul said, "For me to live is Christ, and to die is gain" (Phil. 1:21).

Yes, life is short. What will be your testimony at the end of the way? Will it be a time to weep or a time to rejoice? It depends on what you have done with Christ.

II. ETERNITY IS LONG

In former days the old preachers used two illustrations to tell us of the length of eternity. They would liken this world to a great steel ball. Suppose that an eagle swooped down once every 100 years and barely touched the steel ball with his beak. Then when the world-size steel ball was completely worn out, they said that eternity would have just begun. Then suppose that a sparrow took a drop of water in his beak from the Atlantic Ocean, then hopped across the United States and deposited that drop in the Pacific Ocean. Then suppose he hopped back across the country for another drop from the Atlantic and kept repeating the process. When the sparrow emptied the Atlantic into the Pacific, they said, eternity would have just begun. You may think that these are far-fetched illustrations, but no one can measure the length of eternity.

Here is a man who leaves Christ out of his life. At the judgment of the Great White Throne the Saviour who loved him and died for him is forced to point him down toward hell. Down and down he goes until he lands in the eternal flames. In his suffering he says, "Maybe this will be over in a year." But the year goes by and the fires are as hot as ever, the suffering just as intense. Then he says, "Maybe the suffering will be over in five years." But five years go by and there is no relief. Then he says, "Maybe it will all be over in 100 years." But when the 100 years are over he is still there. He cries out, "How long, how long must I be tormented in these flames?" And the walls resound with the echo, "Forever, forever, forever." Then he realizes that hell never ends.

But here's a man who has lived for Christ, so he goes to heaven. Jesus welcomes him with open arms, saying, "Enter into the joy of thy Lord." He looks around, everything is glorious, peaceful, wonderful, beautiful. He has a perfect body, no pain, no trouble, no problems, no tears. It seems too good to be true. He meets Paul and asks him how long this glorious existence will last. And Paul smiles and says, "Don't you remember that I said we would be with the Lord forever?" Then he meets Peter and asks him how long heaven will last. And Peter says, "It's like I told you, this inheritance will never fade away." Then he goes back to Jesus and the Lord tells him, "It's everlasting life; you are going to enjoy this forever."

Yes, eternity is long, long in hell, oh, the horror of it, long in heaven, oh, the joy of it!

III. Sin Is Black

This world is full of sin, and it has entered your heart and mine. Ever since that old serpent, Satan, brought sin into the Garden of Eden, everyone has been contaminated with the malady of sin. The Bible says that we are born in sin and conceived in iniquity (Ps. 51:5). The Bible says that "all have sinned and come short of the glory of God" (Rom. 3:23). The Bible says that, "like sheep [we] have gone astray; we have turned every one to his own way" (Isa. 53:6).

You can find all kinds of men in the world — white men, black men, red men, brown men, yellow men. You can find rich men and poor men, educated men and ignorant men. But there is one man you can never find. Look for him high and low, near and far, in every corner of the world. But you can never find a man who has not sinned.

What is sin? Let the Bible tell us. It is the "transgression of the law," God's law. On the corner there is a traffic light. You approach it in your car and the light is red. But if you cross that corner then, you transgress man's law. And you must pay the penalty for it. God has some great laws laid down in His book. If you transgress one of these laws, you have sinned.

Then sin is rebellion against God. God says, "Do this." But you say, "I am a free moral agent, I'll do as I please." You have sinned, you have rebelled against God. Then sin is the omission of good. The Bible says, "To him that knoweth to do good, and doeth it not, to him it is sin" (Jas. 4:17). You say, "I never cheat or lie or steal or do any of the evil things of the world." But at the same time you do nothing good for God or man. This is the sin of omission.

But the damning sin is the sin of unbelief. "He that believeth on the Son hath everlasting life: and he that believeth not the Son shall not see life; but the wrath of God abideth on him" (John 3:36). You can find forgiveness for every other sin, but there is no forgiveness for the final rejection of Jesus Christ as Saviour and Lord.

If we could take a trip today through the halls of hell we could talk to the inhabitants of that awful place. We would ask them why they were there. They would not tell us that they were there because they were thieves or drunkards or adulterers. They could have found forgiveness for these sins. No, they would all say, "We are here because we did not put our trust in the Lord Jesus Christ." The rejection of Christ is the damning, dooming sin.

Now sin is deeply rooted in the nature of every human being. Dr. John A. Broadus, a great preacher of another day, was on a trip through the Holy Land. One day he saw a beautiful rosy-cheeked little baby lying in the grass and crying its heart out. He went over to pick up the baby and someone cried out, "Unclean, unclean." He knew what that meant. The baby was the child of leprous parents and the disease was already deep down in the child's body, even though it was a beautiful, rosy-cheeked baby. And many people are like that. They are attractive in appearance, they have sparkling personalities, they have great ability. But deep down in their nature is the disease of sin that will soon crop out and destroy them if they do not come to the healing fountain of Jesus' precious blood. Yes, sin is black.

What is the penalty of sin? The Bible tells us. "The wages of sin is death" (Rom. 6:23). "The soul that sinneth, it shall die" (Ezek. 18:20). "Sin, when it is finished, bringeth forth death" (Jas. 1:15). "And whosoever was not found written in the book of life was cast into the lake of fire" (Rev. 20:15).

What is the remedy for sin? There is only one. When the World's Fair was held in Chicago, a Congress of Religions was a feature of the fair. On a certain day the representatives of the various world religions spoke to a great audience, extolling the merits of their religion. The Mohammedan spoke of the beauties of his religion, and was loudly applauded. The Confucianist spoke of the great teachings of his religion and he was also loudly applauded. Then the Buddhist spoke of the virtues of his religion and received a great ovation. Then Joseph Cook, representing Christianity, stood up to speak. Every eye was upon him, everyone wondered what he would say. How could he match the great things said by these other men? Well, he did not speak so much of the joys and beauties of Christianity. He talked about sin, a familiar subject to his audience. He spoke of how sin ruined nations and destroyed men.

When he reached the climax of his speech he shouted to the Mohammedan, "Do you have any remedy for sin?" The Mohammedan shook his head. He put the same question to the Confucianist and the Buddhist and they both admitted their religions did not provide a remedy for sin. Then he cried out, with the tears streaming down his face, "But Christianity has a remedy for sin, 'The blood of Jesus Christ his Son cleanseth us from all sin.'" And the applause shook the house, he had won the day. Yes, sin is black but there is a remedy for it in the cleansing blood of the Lamb.

IV. Hell Is Certain

Some years ago I preached in a revival near Asheville, North Carolina. A man in the church was a correspondent for one of the Asheville papers. Each night he would take notes on my sermon and send a resume in to the Asheville paper and each day the paper published this write-up of my sermons. One night I preached on "The Bible Truth About Hell." When this sermon was written up in the paper I received a scurrilous letter from a man. He said, "Don't you know that only a backwoods fool would believe in hell? Don't you know that the modern preachers have taken hell out of the Bible?" Yes, I know that, but they haven't destroyed the place. Its fires are as hot as ever.

Now the Bible speaks more about hell than it does about heaven. Why is that? I believe it is because God loves us and wants to warn us, so that we can find the way of escape through His Son. Suppose that you were driving down the highway at seventy-five miles per hour and I knew that a few miles ahead of you the highway had been washed out. I would know that if you drove on your car would be wrecked and you would be killed. What would I do if I were your friend? I would flag you down and say, "Stop, stop, there is danger ahead." Well, the Bible tells us that hell is waiting for all who reject Christ. The Bible warns us about it and the true preacher must also sound out the warning in no uncertain terms.

Hell is a place of separation. It is a place of separation from God and all of His blessings. In that day He will say, "Depart from me, ye cursed, into everlasting fire" (Matt. 25: 41). It also means a separation from your loved ones and friends who have gone to heaven.

Here is a man who has been greatly blessed of God. This man has been given health, strength, prosperity, prestige and the things that count in this world. God gave them to him. But he leaves Christ out of his life. He says, "I can live without God." What happens to him? He goes to a place where he is separated from God and all good things.

Then hell is a place of suffering, suffering that never ends. Listen to some Bible descriptions of the place. "A hell of fire, a place where the fire is not quenched, a furnace of fire, a lake of fire." And the man in Luke 16 said, "I am tormented in this flame." But, you may say, these are just pictures, this is symbolic and figurative language, not to be taken literally. But even if this be so, let me tell you that the real thing is usually worse than the picture.

One night I sat in my living room and watched a forest fire in California pictured on my television set. I could see the leaping flames, I could hear the crackling fire. I was not afraid of it, it was just a picture. I could have put my hand on the picture and not been hurt. But I would not have gone within a mile of the real thing, for that would have been highly dangerous. The real thing was worse than the picture. And if the descriptions of hell in the Bible are just pictures, oh, how much worse the real thing is going to be!

Hell is a place of the lowest association. Listen to Revelation 21:8, "But the fearful, and unbelieving, and the abominable, and murderers, and whoremongers, and sorcerers, and idolaters, and all liars, shall have their part in the lake which burneth with fire and brimstone; which is the second death."

"Oh," you say, "I am not a bad person. I don't belong in that group." But if you leave Christ out of your life you'll be right there in the lake with them, for the second group named are the "unbelievers."

A preacher was holding a meeting in a Virginia town. One night after the service he walked down the street with a deacon and the deacon's daughter, a young lady who was not a Christian. They passed by a carnival and saw a group of drunken men and women in a veritable orgy of sin. The sight was so revolting that they hurried on. Then the preacher said to the young lady, "How would you like to spend eternity with those people?" In anger she said, "What do you mean, sir?" The preacher replied, "Unless you come to Christ that is the kind of people you will live with throughout eternity." The young woman saw the point and soon yielded her heart and life to the Saviour. Yes, hell is a place of the lowest associations.

Hell is a place of memory. As you suffer day by day memory will be working. You'll remember how you went to church and heard a gospel sermon and a gospel invitation. You'll remember how the Holy Spirit pled with you and how you rejected Christ. You'll remember how you could have been saved if only you had turned from your sin to the Saviour. All through the endless ages you'll cry out, "Oh, if I only had, if I only had." Just think of being shut up in hell with your memory forever!

Yes, hell is certain and there is no escape except through the Lord Jesus Christ.

V. HEAVEN CAN BE YOURS

Maybe your mother and father have gone, your other loved ones and friends. Heaven is going to be sweet when you meet them. And there will be no more tears or troubles or sorrows. But the best part of it all is that you'll see Jesus and fall at His feet in gratitude for bringing you home. I have a sermon with the title, "Why Go to Hell When It's So Easy to Go to Heaven?" Yes, it is easy. Jesus said, "I am the way, the truth, and the life: no man cometh unto the Father, but by me" (John 14:6). Just come to Him, this blessed wonderful Saviour and heaven will be yours.

A Texas cowboy with plenty of money made a trip to

London. He was enraptured by Buckingham Palace, where the king lived. So one morning he strode up to the gates, expecting to go right in. But two soldiers stuck out their bayonets and stopped him. He took a one-thousand dollar bill out of his pocket and said to the soldiers, "Take this money, I can pay my way in." But they said, "You can't buy your way into the king's palace. If he invites you in, you can go in free." It's the same way with heaven. You can't pay your way in, but Christ has invited you to come in and you can go in free.

A Christian couple adopted a little orphan girl. She had never had enough of anything in her life. They took her to their beautiful home and said, "This is your home now." They took her to a lovely room and said, "This is your room now, this is your own bed, these are your toys. We are your mommy and daddy now." Then they went down into the kitchen and the good woman poured out a glass of milk and handed it to the little girl. She had never had a whole glass of milk in her life, so she said, "Mommy, how deep can I drink?" And the woman said, "Honey, drink it all and if that isn't enough we'll go to the store and buy some more."

Jesus says the same to you. "Drink deeply," He says, "take all the blessings I have for you here and at the end of the way I'll have a heaven full of good things waiting for you." Who wouldn't want to accept such an invitation as that?

Dear friend, remember these five things. Life is short. Eternity is long. Sin is black. Hell is certain. But heaven can be yours. And one day you must answer to God for the response you make to this message.

Dr. Leslie Weatherhead was a pastor in London. Every day at noon one of his members named Jim came to the church, sat down on the front pew for five minutes, then slipped out. One day the pastor asked Jim about this custom and he said, "The world wears me down, so I sit in the church and bow my head and say, 'Jesus, this is Jim, I need Your help today.' And He always pours new strength into me."

One day the preacher was called to the hospital. Jim was

dying. When the pastor went into the room, Jim asked everyone else to go out. Then he said, "Pastor, when they brought me to the hospital they thought I was unconscious. But I heard them say that I didn't have a chance, that I was going to die. They left me alone for a few minutes, but I felt the presence of someone else in the room. I looked around but didn't see anyone. Then I heard a sweet voice saying, 'Jim, this is Jesus. I have come to take you home. Don't be afraid, Jim, I'll go through the dark valley with you.' Now, preacher, I am not afraid, I am ready to go home with Jesus." And soon he was gone.

Friend, why don't you look up to Him and say, "Jesus, this is Jim or John or Mary or Sue. Come into my heart. Wash away my sins. Save me today." And He'll do it, He'll do it gladly. Then when you come to the end of the way you'll hear Him say, "Jim, John, Mary, Sue, this is Jesus. I've come to take you home. I know the way and I'll see you safely through the dark valley."

Oh, what a Saviour! I plead with you to give Him your heart and life today.

5

THE SCARLET THREAD IN THE WINDOW
Joshua 2:15-21

As Christians read their Bibles from day to day, they usually concentrate on reading the four gospels or the Psalms. Well, there is no finer reading anywhere in all of literature. The gospels picture for us the life and death, the burial and resurrection of our Lord and Saviour, while the Psalms cause us to bow down in worship and rise up in praise of our great God. But for drama, adventure and thrilling stories one must read the Old Testament. In this sermon I want us to think of Rahab and the scarlet thread and how it all relates to our salvation through the blood of our Lord Jesus Christ.

Joshua, the leader of the Israelites after the death of Moses, was preparing for an attack on the city of Jericho. So he sent two men into the city to spy out the land secretly and bring him a report. These two men went to the house of a harlot by the name of Rahab. And the king of Jericho, hearing that these men were in the city, sent a message to Rahab, commanding her to give up to the two men. But Rahab lied to the king. She said, "I don't know where these men are. They came to my house, but about sundown I saw them going out of the city gate, so I suppose they are back with their army by this time." But Rahab had taken the two men up to the roof of her house and had hidden them under some stalks of flax. In the meantime the soldiers of the king were vainly searching for the men.

Now before the two men lay down on the rooftop, Rahab had said to them, "I know how your army is overcoming every city and I know it is because God is with you. I know that in time you will take Jericho. Now I want you to make me a promise. I have been kind to you and I want you to show kindness to my family and me when you take the city. I want you to spare our lives." "All right," said the men, "we promise to save you." Now when they were ready to leave she was going to let them down from the wall on the back side by a scarlet cord, a cord made of many scarlet threads. So one of the men picked up the scarlet thread and said, "This is what you are to do. When we come into the city you are to bind this scarlet thread in the window. Then you are to gather all of your family into your house. When we see the scarlet thread we will save all of those behind it, but if anyone goes out into the street we will not be responsible for his death."

The bargain was made and soon the two spies were on their way back to make their report to Joshua. A few days later the city fell to Joshua. All in the city were destroyed with the edge of the sword, but Rahab and her family were saved because they were hidden behind the scarlet thread. Don't you see the connection between this story and the salvation offered in Christ? Judgment is coming to the world. Great multitudes will be utterly cut off from God and all of His blessings. But Jesus Christ has provided a scarlet thread for all who will trust Him. This thread is His precious blood. Men everywhere are invited to get under the blood today. Then when judgment comes they'll be safe from hell and the wrath of God.

I have a conviction that we ought to have more preaching today about the precious blood of Jesus. The Bible says that "without shedding of blood is no remission" of sin (Heb. 9:22). The Bible says, "The blood of Jesus Christ his Son cleanseth us from all sin" (I John 1:7). Some years ago a certain religious denomination decided that they would cut out of their new songbook every reference to the blood. In this way they were cutting out the heart of the Christian religion.

A certain church was thriving under the leadership of a man who believed the entire Bible and who preached the whole Gospel. The congregation filled the building, souls were being saved and added to the church. Then this pastor was called away to another field and a liberal preacher succeeded him. After a few months one of the members said, "I'm glad our pastor doesn't preach about blood and the cross." Soon the thriving church was declining, the congregation was dwindling, the young people were leaving the church. God does not promise prosperity to a church where the blood of Jesus Christ is treated as an unholy thing. Now let us look into the lessons from this Old Testament story.

I. The Scarlet Thread and Judgment

All those people in Jericho who were not behind the scarlet thread came under the awful judgment of a righteous God. Not one was spared. The king and the slave, the rich and the poor, the good and the bad fell because of their sin and unbelief. In Leviticus we are told that these people were hopelessly depraved. Thus they suffered the consequences of their sin. But Rahab, believing in God, sought mercy and found it.

Today every individual without Christ is facing certain judgment. Every day brings them one day nearer that judgment. When judgment falls they may cry for the rocks and the mountains to fall upon them and hide them from the wrath of the Lamb (Rev. 6:16). But refuge will fail them, God will bring every one of them to the judgment of the Great White Throne.

We notice also that the judgment of Jericho was a judgment unto death. These people were not wounded, they were not taken captive, they met death. And the judgment of the Great White Throne will be a judgment unto death, an everlasting, endless death. The Bible speaks of it as "the second death." You may not fear physical death, the first death, but, oh, the horror of the second death!

The Christian need have no fear of the second death. It is not for him. "There is therefore now no condemnation to them which are in Christ Jesus, who walk not after the flesh, but after the spirit" (Rom. 8:1). But listen to a few Bible descriptions of the second death. It is called the "lake of fire," the "bottomless pit," "outer darkness," the place "where their worm dieth not," the place of "everlasting punishment." It may be true, as some claim, that these are just pictures, that this is symbolic language, but even so, the real thing is always worse than the picture.

He that is born only once will die twice, but he that is born twice, born first of the flesh and then of the Spirit of God, will die only once. Christ has delivered the born-again man from the second death.

We notice also that not all the people in Jericho were saved. Out of a population of several thousand, only about twelve were saved. This does away with universalism, the belief that all people are going to be saved, regardless of their condition before God. The Bible plainly teaches that some shall never be saved. They are condemned because they have not believed on the Lord Jesus Christ (John 3:18).

But someone will say, "God is too good to damn anyone." That is true. He so loved a lost world that He gave His only begotten Son to save it. But when a person tramples that Son under foot, when he leaves Christ out of his life, he damns and dooms himself. Someone will say, "God will never punish His children eternally." But He will punish the children of Satan, and all those who refuse the offer of God's salvation are the children of the devil (John 8:44). No one is a child of God until he is born again. "But as many as received him, to them gave he power to become the sons of God, even to them that believe on his name" (John 1:12).

In II Peter 3:9 we read that God is "not willing that any should perish, but that all should come to repentance." So God makes a way of escape for us through Jesus Christ. It is our own fault if we miss the way. A Christian mother loves her son and wants to see him saved. God loves sinners a million times more than any mother ever loved a son and He has done everything in His power to save them.

I am sure that some religious people were lost when Jericho fell. Religion does not save, only faith in a great God can do that. We are told that in the judgment many shall cry out "Lord, Lord, we did many things in Thy name, let us into glory." But He will say to them, "Depart from Me, I never knew you." Why will He say that to these people? Simply because they are depending on their works alone, they have never been born again.

In the old saloon days there was a saloon in one of our cities with the name over the door, "Christian saloon." Someone went into the saloon one day and said to the proprietor, "Are you a Christian?" And he answered, "No, my name is just Christian." And I am afraid that many people who bear the name "Christian" have never had a saving experience with the Lord Jesus Christ.

No one lives a perfect life. We often backslide, but when we do slip back, we don't have to stay in our sin. The Bible tells us that one who has been born of God does not continue to practice sin. There ought to be a difference between the Christian's life and the sinner's life, and the difference ought to be so marked that all the world can see it.

There is a difference between a hog and a sheep. A hog will wallow in a mud puddle and if you drive him out, he will soon dive into another one. That is his nature. But when a sheep falls into the mud he soon gets up and gets out. And when he comes to the next mudhole, he goes around it. The same thing applies to sinners and Christians. The sinner will sin and then sin again and think nothing of it. But the real Christian is never happy when he sins. As soon as possible he leaves that sin and seeks to avoid it in the future.

We note also that the Jericho sinners who were saved were sinners of the deepest hue. Rahab was a scarlet woman, an outcast, yet she was saved from her sin when she got behind the scarlet thread. And today it is often easier to win a deep-dyed sinner to Christ than to win a person who is morally clean and good. The man who is a base sinner will recognize his need and come to Christ for cleansing and salvation, while the moral man trusts in his goodness and goes to hell.

II. The Scarlet Thread and Salvation

How were these few people saved when judgment fell upon Jericho? They were saved because they got behind the scarlet thread. I can imagine Rahab as she ran to her father's house to tell the family about the judgment to come and how they could be saved. When she knocked on the door her father probably opened the door just halfway and said, "What do you want?" Then she began to pour out her heart to him, telling him of what was going to happen. Then I can imagine him saying, "You're a pretty one to talk to us about God and judgment. You have disgraced our family, you have dragged our good name in the dust. How dare you come and try to tell us what to do?" But Rahab must have been so earnest and so convincing that they finally believed her and followed her home, where they, too, got behind the scarlet thread. Then when judgment fell, when the streets ran red with blood, they surely must have fallen on their knees before Rahab to thank her for bringing them to safety.

Maybe there are some in your home or in your circle of friends who are not Christians. They are in danger of judgment and the second death and hell. Why not go to them to do that, they will look you up in heaven and thank you forever for telling them the way to eternal life.

Now suppose that Rahab had said, "I'm going out on the street, there's a lot of excitement out there." She would have been lost like all the other sinners in Jericho. She had to be behind the scarlet thread to be saved. It isn't enough for you that God loved you, that Christ died for you. In order to be saved, you must make a move. You must come to Jesus in faith to be saved.

This story illustrates clearly the way of eternal salvation. All through the Bible we find that salvation comes only through the shedding of blood (Heb. 9:22). This was true when Israel was in Egypt. Because the blood of a perfect lamb was placed on the door the life of the first-born was spared. And because the perfect Lamb of God shed His precious blood on Calvary's cross we can find forgiveness for sin and eternal life. He has paid the price, He has shed His blood. Now all those who come under the blood are saved and safe forever.

> What can wash away my sin?
> Nothing but the blood of Jesus;
> What can make me whole again?
> Nothing but the blood of Jesus.
> Oh! precious is the flow
> That makes me white as snow;
> No other fount I know,
> Nothing but the blood of Jesus.

General Stonewall Jackson and his Confederate troops were encamped in the Shenandoah Valley of Virginia. They were expecting an attack by the Federal army, so the order was given that no one would be allowed through the lines unless he could give the password. At midnight a poor wounded Confederate soldier approached the lines and was halted by a sentry. He was ordered to give the password or be shot. The boy had been away from the camp all day and did not know the password. Feeling that death was near and remembering how he had been saved by Christ's death on Calvary, he cried out, "The blood, the blood." And the sentry said, "You may pass," for that was the password that night. And our password at the gates of glory must be the same. We are saved by the blood, we are saved when we get behind the scarlet thread.

If I gave you a check for $10,000 today that check would be worthless. But if a Rockefeller or a Henry Ford or some other millionaire would put his name on that check, it would be valuable to you. And if I were to present my works, my goodness, my life to God as an entrance fee into heaven, I would be turned down. But if I turned my life over to Jesus Christ, trusting Him and Him only for my salvation, I would be welcomed into the Holy City.

Now we must not wait too long to get behind the scarlet thread. There is an old Jewish legend which illustrates this point. You will remember that just before God took Israel out of Egypt, He commanded His people to put the lamb's blood on the door that night or the first-born in every home would die. The legend tells us that in one home a little Jewish boy could not sleep. He was not sure that the blood had been put on the door and he knew his life was at stake. He said to his father, "Are you sure that the blood is upon the door?" "Yes," said the father, "my trusted friend put it there. You are all right." But the boy could not sleep and complained to his father again. Then the father said, "Come with me, son, and I'll show you the blood." They went out the door and looked up to see the blood, but it was not there. The father rushed into the house, found the basin of blood and quickly brushed it upon the doorpost and the lintels of the door. As he and his son came back into the house they heard the whir of the wings of the death angel as he flew over the house. The father had acted just in time.

Do not wait to give your heart to Christ. Seek the safety of the scarlet thread today, for you know not what tomorrow may bring. Tomorrow could be too late. We are not saved by baptism, by church membership, by good works or a good life or a large gift. We are saved only as we come by faith to get under the blood. Don't postpone this important matter another minute. There is danger in delay.

When Samuel Hadley was superintendent of the Water Street Mission in New York City, a young man came to the mission one day seeking help. Mr. Hadley gave him a good meal and then asked the boy to tell him something about himself. The boy said, "My home is in Philadelphia. I stole $20.00 from my father and came to New York, hoping that I could find work here. But I have not been able to find work and my money is gone and I don't know what to do."

Mr. Hadley said, "Why don't you go home? I'm sure your father would forgive you and take you back." "But," said the boy, "you don't know my father, he is a hard man, he will never forgive me." But Mr. Hadley said, "Give me his name and address. I'll write him and tell him how you feel, and we'll see what he says." The boy agreed to this and Mr. Hadley wrote the letter.

That letter was delivered to the boy's father in Philadelphia at 9 o'clock the next morning. At 10 o'clock Mr. Hadley received a telegram from the father which read, "Tell my boy that I love him, that I have already forgiven him and that I want him to come home at once."

Oh, a father's love is great but God's love is far greater. If you have never been saved, if you are still under condemnation because of your sin, let me tell you that God loves you with all of His heart. He has done everything necessary to save you, and today His arms are wide open to receive you and save you. What are you going to do about His loving invitation to you? Why not get behind the scarlet thread even now?

6

THE MAN WHO HAD EVERYTHING
BUT THE MAIN THING
Mark 10:17-22

If we could have walked down the pathway of life with Jesus, we would have had many thrilling experiences and would have seen many wonderful things. Let's walk with Him on a certain day. As we walk along, we see a young man dressed in very rich apparel running up to Jesus. He kneels down before the Saviour and says, "Good Master, what must I do to inherit eternal life? What must I do to be sure that I'll go to heaven at the end of the way?"

Now Jesus looked deep down into the soul of that young man and saw what the world couldn't see. The world saw him as rich and young and powerful. But Jesus saw a great hunger in his heart. The young man had so much but he was not satisfied. He longed for the joy and peace that the world could not give him.

The world is full of such people, some are rich and some are not. They are running all over the world, seeking some new thrill. They indulge in all that the world has to offer them, but they are never satisfied. Deep down on the inside there is an aching void and the pleasures of sin and the world soon lose their zest for them, leaving them empty-hearted and hungry-souled. All because they are looking for their satisfaction in the wrong place.

Jesus said to the young man, "Why callest thou me good? there is none good but one, that is, God." Evidently Jesus was seeking to adjust this young man's thinking. All men are sinners, only God is perfectly good. Jesus was not a sinner, as the young man knew. He was perfect goodness, He was God in the flesh. He wanted the young man to know that He was God and that He alone could give eternal life.

Now Jesus tells the young man that he must keep the commandments, and He mentions the commandments which have to do with our relationship to others. He said, "Thou shalt not commit adultery, thou shalt not kill, thou shalt not steal, thou shalt not bear false witness, thou shalt not defraud, thou shalt honor thy father and thy mother." And now we see the young man as he lifts his head in pride saying, "Oh, I have kept these commandments all of my life." Then Jesus said, "You lack one thing, go and sell what you have and give to the poor. Then take up your cross and follow Me."

And right here Jesus put His finger on the sore spot in that young man's life. He was not a thief or a murderer or an adulterer, his sin was that he loved his money and didn't want to give it up. He was breaking the first commandment, "Thou shalt have no other gods before me." And until we turn from our sin to God through Christ there is no salvation for us.

Now look at the young man. He turns and sadly walks away. He was not willing to give up his sin, his love for money. As he goes away we can see the sorrow in every step. His head is bowed and his shoulders are stooped. You are looking at a man who has committed spiritual suicide, who has rejected the only salvation. You are looking at a man on his way to hell. I call him the man who had everything but the main thing.

I. What Did the Young Man Have?

1. *He had wealth.* Many people think that money is everything. They say, "If I only had money, I would be truly happy." But some people with money have been absolutely

miserable. The name of Rothschild is synonymous with wealth. When someone asked the elder Rothschild if money brought happiness, he replied, "No, I only wish it did, for I know many people who are rich, but they are not happy, for wealth does not bring happiness."

Some years ago I heard a preacher say, "When I was a young man I worked beside another young man for a dollar per day. The years went by and the other man became a millionaire, but I became a preacher and remained poor. After a lapse of twenty-five years I met my old friend again, now a millionaire. I asked him if he was as happy now as he was when we worked for a dollar per day. He said, 'No, I am not. The responsibilities and obligations and burdens laid on me by my wealth far outweigh the happiness it has brought. I don't have the peace and joy in my heart that I had when we worked side by side for a dollar per day.'"

A few years ago Mr. Robert R. Young was president of the New York Central Railroad. He had a big salary, several homes, all that money could buy. But one day he went to an upstairs room in his Palm Beach home and blew his brains out. His money did not bring happiness.

Now the Bible does not condemn money, but the love of it. Money can do many wonderful things for God and man, if it is made honestly and used rightly. On the other hand, although it can buy many things, it cannot buy happiness on this earth or a home in heaven. One of the queens of England, as she lay dying, cried out, "Millions for an inch of time." But when the time comes for you to go all the money on earth will not buy you another minute or another opportunity to be saved.

2. *He had morality.* He could say, "I have lived a clean life all of my days." It is fine if you can say that, but your morality, your personal goodness, will not save you.

A dear Christian woman, one of my parishioners, died very suddenly. Her husband was not a Christian. After the funeral service I found an opportunity to talk to him. I said, "Your wife has gone to heaven now, maybe this is God's call for you to become a Christian." He looked me straight in the eye and said, "I want you to know that I am as clean as anyone in this county, and the plate never passes by but that I put something in it." And the poor man thought that his clean life and his infrequent gifts would atone for a life of sin. You may be the cleanest man in the city, but your morality will not save you.

This young man in our text would have made a good neighbor and a fine citizen. The good people would say, "Let's elect him as our mayor." If a woman had a marriageable daughter, she would have said, "I hope she can marry a man like that." If he had been a member of one of our churches we would have said, "He would serve well as the chairman of our board of deacons."

But human goodness without Christ is not true goodness. If a man tells me that he is a good man but has never accepted Christ, I know he is not good according to the best meaning of the word. Suppose you tell me about a certain man. You say, "He's a wonderful man. He is good to his family and friends. He lives a clean life, he helps all those in need. He is at the forefront of every good cause, he gives liberally to every worthy enterprise." I would say, "He surely must be a good man." Then you say, "But I can't understand the way he treats his mother. She is in the county poorhouse. He is rich but he gives her no money. He won't even let her see her grandchildren." Then I say, "You call this man a good man, but since you have told me how he treats his mother, I say to you that he is not a good man."

So how can we say that any man is a good man who lives a good life and is good to everybody, if that man rejects and tramples under foot the Saviour who died for him? He is guilty of committing the blackest sin this side of hell. A man who rejects Christ is not a good man.

3. *He had youth.* Oh, what a premium we put on youth today! A church doesn't want to call a man over forty years of age, and the world of business demands men who are young and vigorous.

Well, the time to come to Christ is when you are young. Of all the unsaved people in America between twenty-five and thirty-five years of age, we are told that only one in five thousand will ever be saved. Of all the unsaved people in America between thirty-five and forty-five years of age, only one in twenty-five thousand will ever be saved. Of all the unsaved people in America between forty-five and fifty-five years of age, only one in eighty thousand will ever be saved.

Solomon said, "Remember now thy Creator in the days of thy youth, while the evil days come not, nor the years draw nigh, when thou shalt say, I have no pleasure in them" (Eccl. 12:1). He was simply saying that if you don't live for Christ when you are young, you'll have nothing good to look back upon. The devil has no happy old people. I don't say that older people cannot be saved, but the longer you put off the matter of your salvation, the harder it becomes to make a decision.

4. *He had social rank.* Oh, what some of our people will do to rise up in the social world! They'll give up their service for the Lord, they'll turn their backs upon the church, they'll neglect their families, they'll spend money they don't have, just to gain some social recognition. The height of their ambition is to get their pictures in the paper or to be elected to some office.

Dr. J. Wilbur Chapman was conducting a meeting in a certain city and a rich society woman came to hear him preach. She had entertained the most prominent people of America and the royalty of Europe in one of her homes. But that night she was convicted of her sin and saw her need of Christ. She want forward and surrendered her heart and life to Jesus. One week later she said to Dr. Chapman, "I have had a full and interesting life. I have entertained the greatest people of America and the royalty of Europe, but I want to tell you that I have had more happiness and peace packed in this one week since I met Christ than in all the other years that I have lived." You see, Christ means more than a high social life.

5. *He had a form of religion.* He fasted and tithed and went through all the forms of religion, but this did not

satisfy his inner hunger. And the forms of religion will leave you cold, unless Christ is in your heart.

Dr. E. Stanley Jones said, "For twelve years I have sat around the table with the leaders of all the world religions. I have heard all they have to offer and I say that Jesus only has the remedy for the miseries of mankind." It isn't religion that satisfies and saves, it is a personal relationship with the Son of God.

6. *He had good sense.* He came to Jesus at the right time, when he was young. Billy Sunday said that some men burned the candle of life out for the devil and then blew the smoke in God's face at the end of the way.

7. *This young man had the right spirit,* the spirit of humility. He came and knelt before Jesus. That's the manner in which a sinner must come to Jesus, not in his pride or self-righteousness, but in humility. "Except ye . . . become as little children, ye cannot enter the kingdom of God" (Matt. 18:3).

8. *This young man came seeking the right thing,* eternal life. You may search for wealth, for health, for an education or for many other things. But the most important search in life is the search for God and eternal life. And God tells us that when we seek Him with the whole heart we will find Him.

9. *And he came to the right place.* He came to Jesus, he came to headquarters. If you need spiritual help don't try to find it in the world. Come to Jesus and the Word of God. So we see what this young man had. He had wealth, he had morality, he had youth, he had social prominence, he had a form of religion, he had good sense. But Jesus said, "One thing thou lackest." You may have everything that the world can offer, but if you don't have Jesus Christ you lack everything. "For what shall it profit a man, if he shall gain the whole world, and lose his own soul?" (Mark 8:36).

II. What Was the Young Man Offered?

1. *He was offered a Saviour.* Jesus did not argue theology with him. He simply offered Himself. He said, "Come and

follow me." What a friend we have in Jesus! He is the solution to every problem, the answer to every question, the satisfaction for every need.

Some years ago I held a meeting in Rome, Georgia. Just across the street from the church there was a fire station. The captain of the fire station was not a Christian. He came over to the services two or three nights. Then one night, at the close of the service, the pastor and I took him back into the study to talk to him about his salvation. That night he gave his heart to Jesus. The next day he had to go and fight a disastrous warehouse fire. When he returned he came over to the church and said to us, "I used to be afraid of fires like that. I was afraid of the burning roof or the walls falling in on me. But," he said, "today I had no fear for I knew that my Best Friend was with me."

Yes, He is the Best Friend one can ever have. He comes to save you, to wash away your sin, to take you into His family, to write your name down in the Lamb's Book of Life. He comes to walk by your side every day and to take you to heaven at the end of the way. The Bible tells us that Jesus loved this young man, He wanted to save him. He loves you, too. He wants to be your Saviour.

In the old days in North Carolina a certain preacher would often visit a liquor dealer's house, for the man's wife was a devoted Christian and a member of his church. Always, when the preacher was leaving the man's house, this liquor dealer would follow him to the gate, press some money into his hand and say, "Preacher, use that money where it will do the most good." One day when that happened the preacher held on to the man's hand and said, "You're a fine man, you're too good a man to go to hell. I begrudge the devil your soul." The man went back into his house and said to his wife, "That preacher said that I was a fine man and too good to go to hell, and that he begrudged the devil my soul. Tell me how to be saved." His wife soon led him to Christ, he gave up his liquor business and became a faithful Christian and church member.

There are many fine people in this world, good people,

clean people, generous people. They are too good to go to hell, but there is no hope for them if they will not come to Christ.

2. *He was offered a cross.* To him the cross would be the giving up of his money, the thing he loved best. So he said "no" to Jesus. His money bags stood between him and the Saviour and they shall haunt him throughout eternity. What is it that stands between you and Christ? Give it up or it will take you to hell. Give it up and Christ will give you something a million times better.

Gypsy Smith held a meeting in Boston and hundreds were saved. On the last night of the meeting a woman came up to speak to Mr. Smith, bringing her five-year-old boy with her. She said, "Mr. Smith, I want my boy to have the privilege of shaking hands with the man who has held the greatest meeting Boston has ever known." Mr. Smith very graciously reached down to shake hands with the boy, but the little fellow held out his left hand. Mr. Smith said, "No, give me your right hand." The boy reached out his right hand but it was doubled up in a fist. Seeing that others were waiting to speak to him Mr. Smith pried the boy's fingers apart. And in the boy's hand there were three little marbles. The boy didn't care about shaking hands with the great preacher, he just wanted to hold on to his marbles.

Jesus comes to give us His salvation and to guide us through life and death and into heaven. But some people care not for Him or anything He has to offer. They are holding on to some sin, some habit, some pleasure that is dear to them. They are not willing to give up these things in order that Christ might fill their lives with the true riches of redemption and glory.

3. *He was offered a home in heaven.* Jesus told him that if he would follow Him he would have treasure in heaven. He was simply promising him that when he came to the end of the way he would not go down to hell, but up to heaven, where eternal joys would be his, where all tears would be wiped away and where he would live in bliss forever. Oh,

how sweet it will be at life's end to hear Jesus say "I've been waiting for you, I have everything ready. Come on in and enter into the joy of thy Lord." Will that be your lot, or will you sink into hell when life's little day is over?

III. WHAT DID THE YOUNG MAN DO?

1. *He rejected the only Saviour and forfeited eternal life.* He wanted eternal life, but he wanted to be saved on his own terms, through his good deeds and good life. When I first entered the ministry I heard preachers say that many people wanted to be saved by their works. And I said, "No, they are wrong, everybody knows that they can be saved only through faith in Christ." But I have learned that these preachers were right. Go out and talk to any lost man about his salvation and he'll begin to tell you about the good life he lives, of his good works and generous gifts. But no one can be saved by these things. "Salvation is of the Lord," not of ourselves.

There are two kinds of religion. One is spelled "d-o, do," which tells you all you must do to merit salvation and eternal life. But the Christian religion is spelled "d-o-n-e, done," which means that Christ has done everything necessary to save us.

> Jesus paid it all,
> All to Him I owe,
> Sin had left a crimson stain,
> He washed it white as snow.

So the young man turned away from Jesus. It was all over in a minute, his decision was made, his doom was sealed. In the twinkling of an eye he decided for hell instead of heaven. In the twinkling of an eye you can decide for heaven instead of hell.

2. *He walked away in sorrow.* No wonder, no wonder. He had made the most awful mistake of his life. He is not laughing, he is grieving, he is on the way to hell.

If I had met him on the street I would have said, "Friend, what's the trouble? You look downhearted and dejected."

Then, after he had told me what had happened, I would have grasped him by the arm and said, "Come on, let's go back and find Jesus. He is a great compassionate, forgiving Saviour. I'm sure He'll still save you and give you eternal life." But then he would have jerked away from me and said, "No, I can't do it, I can't give up my sin." And then he would have told me good-by.

Oh, the tragedy of it all! The tragedy of it then and the tragedy of it now. But on every side men are holding on to their sin and giving up eternal life. Let me close with two contrasting pictures.

Just before a young Texas man went away to the university a preacher urged him to accept Christ as his Saviour. "Preacher," the young man said, "I am going to the university and get my law degree. Then I'll come home, give my heart to the Lord, join your church and live an active Christian life." The preacher tried to persuade him not to postpone the matter, but he said, "That's my program, preacher, and I'm going to stick to it." When he would come home at Christmas or vacation time he would say, "Don't bother me, preacher. You know my plans." The time came for graduation and the young man was critically ill in the university hospital. Someone else had to go forward and receive his diploma. They brought the diploma out to the hospital and pinned it to the young man's pillow, and he died the next day. He won his degree, but he lost his soul.

Dr. W. H. Major was pastor of the Capitol Avenue Baptist Church in Atlanta. He baptized me, married my wife and me, and ordained me to the ministry. When he died my wife and I went back to Atlanta for the funeral. The church was packed with Dr. Major's members and friends. Several preachers paid a marvelous tribute to this good man of God. Then, as the casket was wheeled down the aisle and out toward the hearse, the organist played very softly, "It is well, it is well with my soul."

Oh, when I come to the end of the way, I want it to be that way with my soul, don't you? Come to Jesus and it will be.

7

PREPARE TO MEET THY GOD

Amos 4:12

Some years ago I conducted a revival in a small South Georgia town. On a Sunday morning I preached on my text, "Prepare to meet thy God." When I pressed the invitation for people to make their preparation for meeting the Lord there was no response. I felt that the service had been a failure. But the day wore away and we came back to the Lord's house for the evening service. I preached on another subject and gave the gospel invitation. A man about thirty-five years of age came forward to receive Christ as his personal Saviour. At the close of the service he said, "I was in church this morning and heard you preach on 'Prepare to meet thy God.' I was deeply convicted of my sin. I went home but I did not feel like eating my Sunday dinner. I could not get away from your text. I tried to read the Sunday paper, I did everything to get away from the thought of meeting God, but it was all in vain. So I have come tonight to give my heart to Christ, so that I will be ready to meet God."

If you forget everything I say in this sermon, every Scripture I quote, every illustration I use, I pray that you'll not be able to forget this text, "Prepare to meet thy God." I pray that you'll make that preparation even now by trusting

Christ as your personal Saviour. There are only five little words in this text, but how important they are. They contain both a warning and a command. We are warned that some day we must meet God, we are commanded to prepare for that meeting. God is the only one who knows all about us. He knows about every word we've spoken, every work of our hands, every thought of our minds. He knows about our sinful lives and knowing all of this He says, "Prepare, prepare to meet thy God."

We prepare for everything else. We prepare to make a living through education and training. We prepare to take care of our family by furnishing them a home. We prepare for a wedding in the family. We prepare for retirement through pension plans and investments. We prepare for the future of our loved ones by purchasing life insurance. We prepare for burial by purchasing a cemetery lot. So many people prepare for all of these things, but they neglect the matter of preparing to meet God. They forget that some day they must meet Him and give an account of their lives.

I. We Are Not Ready to Meet God in Our Natural State

The Bible says that we are born in sin and conceived in iniquity; that we go astray as soon as we are born, speaking lies; that we have all sinned and come short of the glory of God. Surely then we are not ready to meet God until some change takes place, until some preparation is made.

There is such a difference between us and God. He is perfect, sinless, stainless, high and holy and altogether righteous. But we are sinners. We live in sin, we walk in sin, we talk in sin, we think in sin. Surely such vile creatures as we are can never face a holy and righteous God. Something must be done, we must prepare to meet God.

Before Jesus went away He said, "I go to prepare a place for you" (John 14:2). Heaven is a prepared place, but it is for prepared people only. Heaven has already been prepared for us, but are we prepared for heaven? Just think of it, some day we must stand before the great God of heaven and earth. Are you ready?

II. WE MUST MEET GOD IN THIS LIFE

God has certain unchangeable laws. We call them "the laws of nature." If we violate these laws we come face to face with the judgments of God. We must pay and pay dearly for every violation of God's laws. "Whatsoever a man soweth, that shall he also reap" (Gal. 6:7). A man says, "I am a free human being, I will live as I please and it's nobody's business but mine." Then one day he comes face to face with the consequences of his sinful life and learns that God will not be mocked, that he must pay the penalty of his evil deeds. Yes, we sin and the days go by and we forget all about it. Then one day something happens, and we remember and say, "God is paying off."

Joseph's brothers mistreated him and sold him into slavery. Then twenty-two years go by and Joseph is the big man down in Egypt. When a famine forced his brothers to come down into Egypt to buy grain, they were faced with problems and troubles. Then one of them wisely said, "I know why this trouble has come upon us. We cruelly mistreated our brother, Joseph, and now we must meet our sin again. God is paying off."

There is only one consolation here for the Christian who has sinned. He can judge himself, recognize his sin and confess it unto God for "He is faithful and just to forgive us our sins and to cleanse us from all unrighteousness" (I John 1:9).

III. WE MUST MEET GOD IN LIFE'S RESPONSIBILITIES

A woman lay dying in the hospital. As her husband stood by the bedside she said to him, "God has given us a baby as a gift of love. But I will not be here to bring up the baby in the right way. So I charge you to care for him, to teach him the way of God, and to bring him to meet me some day in heaven." What a responsibility! These responsibilities are thrust upon us every day and we must account to God for the way we handle them.

One responsibility which is ours is the responsibility of not only being a consecrated Christian, but also a faithful church member. You may belong to many clubs and organizations, you may enjoy many high privileges, but there is in life no higher privilege than that of belonging to a New Testament Church. And with that privilege comes a responsibility to be faithful and active and generous in your church.

Some years ago I held a meeting in a small town and my singer visited a family and sought to get them to move their membership to the local church. The man of the house said, "We like the church, we like the pastor and the people, but we haven't moved our membership because we don't know whether or not we are going to live here permanently." "How long have you lived here?" asked the singer. And the man replied, "Twenty years." Just think of it! Twenty years of service that could have been given to the Lord. Twenty years of setting the wrong example before his family and the world. God calls men to account for such neglect.

But let me give you a contrasting picture. When I was in the seminary I served as pastor of a small church some distance from the school. I knew almost everyone in the community. One Sunday morning when I reached the pulpit I saw some people in the church whom I did not know. A man sat near the front with his wife, four boys and a girl. I thought that they were simply visitors in the little town. But when I had preached and given the invitation they came forward to move their membership to that church. They had moved to the community on Thursday, they joined the church at the first opportunity and became faithful and active members. More than twenty years went by and I had moved to another part of the country and had lost sight of that family. Then I had a nice letter from the father, telling me that his sons were serving God as preachers and that his daughter had married a fine Christian man and was active in her church. Now do you think that would have happened if the man had kept his family out of the church for twenty years?

I have often seen this sign in churches, "What kind of a church would this church be if every member were just like me?" If every member of our churches were like some members, we would have no churches, for some members live and act as if they never heard of God. But if all of our members were like some other members, we would have the most glorious churches in the world, doing a mighty work for the Lord Jesus.

Some of our members are like Easter "bunnies." They hop out to church on Easter Sunday and turn their backs upon the church and God for the rest of the year. But they must give an account to God for the way they handled this and every other responsibility.

IV. We Must Account to God for the Way We Use Our Influence

Every one of us is casting a shadow. It is either for good or for bad. We lift people up or we push them down. "No man liveth unto himself." "No man is an island." Now mothers and fathers have the strongest influence of all. Your children are going to be what you have influenced them to be. Maybe you often ask the question, "What will my boy or girl be when they grow up?" Well, that depends largely upon you, upon the example you set, upon the influence you exert.

Some years ago I was in a meeting in Virginia. At the close of the service one night a tall, nice-looking man came up to speak to me. He had a little boy with him. He asked me if I recognized him and I said, "I'm sorry, but I don't believe I do. I meet so many people that it's hard to remember them all." Then he told me his name and I remembered. We had played together when we were little boys back in a small southern town. I told him how glad I was to see him after all the years had gone by, then I said, "Cliff, are you a Christian?" He answered, "No, but I'm bringing up my little boy to be a Christian." And I had to say to him, "Old friend, you can't do that. Unless you are a Christian yourself, you can't influence that boy for Christ." And how true that is. There is so much power in our influence.

In one of my churches we had a couple who were highly critical of everything about the church. They criticized the Sunday school teachers, the deacons, the choir, the preacher. In fact they had "roast preacher" for dinner every Sunday. Now the tragedy of it was that they had a teenage boy and their criticisms were often in his presence. That's the worst thing a parent can do. And the time came when we tried to help that boy in a spiritual way, but we found it impossible to lead him over the criticisms and the influence of that critical pair of church members.

One morning a man was walking to his office through the snow. Hearing a sound behind him, he looked back and saw that his small son was stretching his steps and trying to walk where his father had walked. "What are you doing, son?" asked the father. And the little boy answered, "Nothing, I'se just walking in daddy's tracks." The man sent the boy back home but he could not get the thought out of his mind that his little son was "walking in daddy's tracks." He went to his office, locked the door, then got down on his knees and prayed, "Lord, if my little boy is going to walk in my tracks, please help me to make the right kind of tracks." Yes, we have an influence, somebody is going to walk in our tracks. And we must answer to God as to how we use that influence.

V. We Must Meet God in Death

Let me give you two contrasting experiences which were mine in my pastorate. An unsaved man whose wife was a member of my church had been quite ill. One of my deacons and I went out to see him one night. We wanted to talk to him about his relationship to God, hoping that we could win him to Christ. He came to the door when we arrived and said, "I've had a hard day and am going to bed. Please come back some other night." We went back a week later, quite early in the evening. But his wife came to the door and said, "He has already gone to bed, come back some other night." We returned a week later and he again came to the door. He said, "I know what you want to see me about and I do want to talk to you. But I'm not feeling very well tonight. Please come back again." We promised that we would.

Some days later I received a call from the hospital, telling me that he was there seriously ill. I rushed over to the hospital, arriving there in ten minutes. But when I went to his room even the bed had been removed. I feared the worst, so I went to the waiting room and found his wife and daughter there, weeping. In those ten minutes his soul had gone out to face God. I wonder if he was ready.

Now here is the other picture. Brother Swenson, who had been a missionary in Argentina for thirty-three years, came to our city upon retirement and we placed him on our staff as church visitor. He was very fine and faithful, especially in visiting the older members of our congregation. Our people loved him very much. One afternoon I conducted the funeral of one of our members, but Brother Swenson was not present. He nearly always attended these funerals, for he had, in nearly every case, visited the one who had died. But as he wasn't present I thought that he was out visiting somewhere. I went on down to the cemetery for the burial and on the way back I called my secretary. She told me that Brother Swenson had died suddenly in the doctor's office. I rushed to the doctor's office and was there about twenty minutes after the dear good man had died. The doctor told me that Brother Swenson had come in and said only one sentence, then had fallen over, dead. As I saw Brother Swenson lying there on the doctor's table and later as I conducted his funeral service, I felt that I knew where he was. He was in the presence of Jesus. He had made his preparation for meeting God.

One hundred short years from now all of us will be gone. We'll be somewhere in eternity, in heaven or in hell. Are you ready to meet God with the life you are now living? Many a man had gone to church and, under the Spirit's power, has been deeply convicted for sin. He has said, "Some day I'll do something about this matter. Some day I'll give my heart to Jesus." But the days go by and he neglects the most important thing in life. Then one day death creeps up and takes him away and he goes out to a Christless eternity, although he had planned to make spiritual preparation "some day." Oh, death is the common lot of all. "It is appointed unto man once to die, but after this the judgment." (Heb. 9:2)

VI. WE MUST MEET GOD AT THE JUDGMENT

Beyond this vale of tears we must all stand before the Judgment Bar of Almighty God. You can go before a judge in this world and plead "not guilty." But you can't plead "not guilty" when you stand before God. He has all the evidence, He knows all the facts. And He has the power to pronounce the sentence of eternal doom upon all who have trampled His Son under foot.

Yes, it will be an awful moment when the sinner stands before God. But listen, there is One who offers to stand for you. Jesus Christ, the strong Son of God, is ready to take your place and clear your name before God. You have only to accept Him as your Saviour and He will gladly become your Advocate.

A preacher dreamed that he died and stood before the Judgment Bar. God asked him if he had always been clean in life and he had to say, "No." He was asked if he had always been true and he had to say, "No." He was asked if he had always been honest and he had to say, "No." Then be bowed his head to receive the condemnation of a righteous God. But he said that as he bowed his head a bright light shone before him and he looked up to see Jesus coming to stand beside him. Jesus looked up to God and said, "Father, I know he hasn't always been clean and true and honest, but down there on the earth he stood for me and now I come to stand for him in heaven." And the preacher said that he awoke from his dream, grateful that he had a Saviour to stand for him at the courts of heaven. Do you have this Saviour?

VII. How to Prepare to Meet God

The world tells you that you can be saved by your good life, your good works, your generous gifts. But "let God be true and every man a liar." This is not God's way of salvation. A wreck occured on a certain railroad line and when they were able to pull the engineer out of his cab, he said, as he held up a yellow slip of paper, "Somebody gave me the wrong orders, somebody gave me the wrong orders." So I must give you God's orders, God's way to obtain eternal life. If some theologian had composed this plan, we could say that he could be mistaken. But this is God's way, as found in God's Book.

First, there is repentance, a Godly sorrow for sin which causes you to turn your back on that sin. There is absolutely no substitute for repentance. The bad man must repent, but so must the good man. If a man of eighty came forward to be saved, I would have to say to him, "Old man, with a lifetime of sin behind you, you must repent of all your sin if you want to be saved." Then if a boy of twelve came for the same purpose, I would have to say to him, "Little boy, with a few years of sin behind you, you must repent of that sin if you want to be saved." We must all begin with repentance — that is the first step to God. The long-necked giraffe and the tiny snail went into the ark through the same door. And the good sinner and the bad one, the rich sinner and the poor one, the educated sinner and the ignorant one, must all come to God, first of all, through repentance.

Then there is faith in Christ, a personal trust in Him as Lord and Saviour. "As many as received him, to them gave he power to become the sons of God, even to them that believe on his name" (John 1:12). "He that believeth on the Son hath everlasting life: and he that believeth not the Son shall not see life; but the wrath of God abideth on him" (John 3:36).

Now if a person genuinely repents of his sin and really and truly puts his trust in Christ the Saviour, he will not hesitate to confess Him before the world. This will prove that He has been saved. Romans 10:10 says, "With the heart man believeth unto righteousness; and with the mouth confession is made unto salvation." Matthew 10:32 says, "Whosoever therefore shall confess me before men, him will I confess also before my Father which is in heaven."

VIII. When Should This Preparation Be Made?

The Bible tells us that "now is the accepted time; behold, now is the day of salvation" (II Cor. 6:2). "Boast not thyself of tomorrow; for thou knowest not what a day may bring forth" (Prov. 27:1). We are told also that we are not to harden our hearts when we hear His voice. Haven't you heard that voice? Hasn't God spoken to you today? Don't you feel your need of Him?

An eagle was flying above the Niagara River when his keen eye spied a dead chicken on a block of ice that was floating down the river. He swooped down, planted his feet firmly on the block of ice and began to enjoy a good meal. Soon the ice began to float faster down the stream and the eagle knew his time was limited, that soon the ice would go over the falls. But he was not afraid, he was king of the birds, he had flown over the falls many times and he could do it again. Soon he heard the roar of the falls, but decided to take one more bite before flying away. In a moment he spread his mighty wings to fly, but he could not move. As he had delayed his feet had sunk into the ice and he could not extricate himself. The block of ice plunged over the falls, carrying the screaming eagle to his death on the rocks below.

This is but a little story but it illustrates what many men do. They are enjoying their sin for a season. They know that someday they must die and they say, "Before that time comes I'll give up my sin, I'll give my heart to Jesus, I'll get ready to meet God." But they become so entrenched in their sin that they come to the time when it has a death grip on them and they cannot leave it to come to God. And so they die in their sin.

A dear old preacher held a meeting in a tabernacle in a sawmill town. One night a fine strong young man came forward and gave his heart to Christ. The next morning he sang happily at his work, for he had found the Lord. No one can be truly happy if he is not a Christian. But just before noon there was an accident and he was badly injured. They rushed him over to the little hospital and the doctor came in to examine him. He had to tell the young fellow that he only had a little while to live. "That's all right," said the young man, "but I would like to see that old preacher before I die." They sent for the preacher and he came and stood by the boy's bedside. The boy looked up and said, "Preacher, I know I'm not going to live, but I am not afraid. Last night in your service I gave my heart to Jesus. I really meant it. This morning I have been happy in Him. As I die now I want you to know that it is all well with me. I am not afraid, for I am simply trusting Jesus and I know He will take me to heaven."

How will it be with you when you come to the end of the way? Prepare to meet thy God.

8

RISE UP AND WALK

John 5:1-9

One night a drunkard sat at a table in a bar, drinking with his companions. Soon his wife came in and set a covered dish before him, saying, "Jack, you seem too busy to come home for supper, so I brought your supper to you." As she left the saloon the man's companions roared with laughter. Jack then invited them to have supper with him. He removed the cover and found the dish to be empty, but in it was a note which said, "Jack, I hope you enjoy your supper. This is just what the children and I have at home."

Yes, Satan's dishes are always empty. But Christ fills the Christian's dishes with the best things for time and eternity. In this Bible story we learn how He blessed a man who had been sick and needy for thirty-eight years. The Jews were having a big feast in Jerusalem, so Jesus went into the city. I imagine that He walked all around, seeking someone whom He could help. Soon He came to the pool of Bethesda. There were five porches around the pool and they were filled with the sick, the blind, the halt, the withered. They were not in order as we would find them today in a hospital, they were lying around on old rags or quilts. One man had been there for thirty-eight long years. How much he must have suffered! Jesus asked him if he wanted to be healed. He replied that no man ever came to put him in the healing waters. So Jesus said, "Rise, take up thy bed, and walk." And the poor man, after thirty-eight years of suffering, rose up and walked. His health had been restored, his life had been transformed, and he did not hesitate to testify that Jesus had wrought the miracle. In this story we find three meaningful facts.

  I. THE CONDITION OF THE MAN
  II. THE COMING OF THE SAVIOUR
  III. THE COMMAND OF CHRIST

I. THE CONDITION OF THE MAN

1. *He was helpless.* Probably someone brought him to the pool every morning and came after him every night, but all the day long he lay there in a helpless condition. Now this is a picture of a lost sinner. He is helpless, he can't do anything to save himself. And isn't that the condition of all of us? Without Christ we can do nothing. Yet Paul said, "I can do all things through Christ which strengtheneth me" (Phil. 4:13). All of our talent, all of our wisdom, all of our personality is as nothing unless Christ is in it.

I have known men who had great ability, sparkling personalities, radiant friendliness, yet their lives were not counting for the most because they did not know Christ. What we could do if we were fully surrendered to Him! So we as Christians must be careful to see that Christ has all of us. If not, we are nothing. But this man, primarily, was a picture of a sinner, in that he was unable to help himself.

2. *He was hopeless.* Surely when he first came to the pool of Bethesda, he must have had great hopes of getting well. At the end of the first year he may have said, "Surely I'll be all right by this time next year." But the years came and went and he soon gave up hope. No life is so bleak as the one which has no hope. The man without Christ has no hope. There is no future for him. There await him only a cold grave and a hot hell.

But, thank God, the Christian has hope. He has hope that God will take care of him and his loved ones. He has hope that God will comfort him in sorrow. He has hope that God will be with him when he comes to the "dark valley of the shadow of death." He has hope that God will take him home at the end of the way.

3. *He was friendless.* A friend is one who knows all about you and still loves you. A friend is one who comes in when all the world goes out. But the best Friend is Jesus. He is a Friend who sticks closer than a brother. He is a Friend who will never forsake us in spite of our sins. Now this man didn't know it, but the One who stood by the poolside had come to be his Friend.

So here is the man, hopeless, helpless, friendless. Jesus is the only One who can help him. "Man's extremity is God's opportunity." And when we come to the end of our resources, when we feel that the whole world is against us, Jesus is very near. All we need to do is to call upon Him and He will help us.

II. The Coming of the Saviour

We read that Jesus saw him and knew he had been there a long time. Yes, He sees and knows all about us. In the Old Testament we read, "Thou God seest me." He sees us in the brightness of the midday and the darkness of the midnight. He sees us when we sin. "Be sure your sin will find you out" (Num. 32:23).

But here is a comforting thought. When we are in trouble or sorrow He sees us also. You may think that you don't count with God, that you are simply one small person among the millions on earth, but you are someone in His sight. The One who notes the sparrow's fall looks upon your distress and is always ready to fly to your relief.

Now Jesus proceeds to heal this man. The man had been looking to the pool for his healing and had been bitterly disappointed, but here is the Great Physician ready to do all for him that he needs. Here is where the religious world divides today. Some people look to their own works for salvation. Some look to Christ and Him alone for salvation. They realize that "there is none other name under heaven given among men, whereby we must be saved" (Acts 4:12).

Some people say, "He has done it all." Others say, "I must do something." Some say, "Jesus paid it all." Others say, "I must pay my way to heaven." But Jesus looked on this man, loved him, had compassion on him, and healed him in the twinkling of an eye.

III. The Command of Christ

He said to the man, "Rise, take up thy bed, and walk." He says the same thing to us. After we have been saved we are to not remain seated, we are to rise up and walk for Jesus. Suppose that you were in a burning building and a fireman rushed in and saved your life, but suppose that it cost him his life. Wouldn't you go to his funeral, wouldn't you send some flowers, wouldn't you show your appreciation in some way? Surely you would. Well, Jesus has saved you from the burning pits of hell. Shouldn't you acknowledge it in some way?

What does He call upon us to do?

1. *He calls us to rise up and walk in an open confession of Him.* If we have been truly saved we will do it. If we have had the tremendous experience of sins forgiven, we will be glad to confess Him before all the world. "For with the heart man believeth unto righteousness; and with the mouth confession is made unto salvation" (Rom. 10:9, 10). "Whosoever therefore shall confess me before men, him will I confess also before my Father which is in heaven" (Matt. 10:32).

I have known people to make a confession of faith in the hospital or in the home, but they stopped right there. They never came out on the Lord's side. They never came to church to confess Him publicly. They went on living in the same old way. I doubt if their conversion is genuine. Right after the verse which tells us to confess Him as our Saviour and Lord we read these words, "Whosoever believeth on him shall not be ashamed" (Rom. 10:11). If you have been truly saved you will rise up and walk in an open, unashamed confession of Christ.

2. *He calls us to rise up and walk into the baptismal waters.* When a person has been really saved, his first impulse and desire is to follow Christ in baptism. This is not something that brings salvation, this is a matter of obedience which follows salvation. Let the new-born Christian go to the Bible, read about the baptism of Jesus and follow His example.

3. *He calls us to rise up and walk in a faithful church membership.* Nothing in the world can benefit a Christian as much as a faithful relationship to a gospel church. And how wonderful it would be if all of our church members were faithful. Think of the added spiritual power our churches would have. Think of the many souls that would be won to Christ. Think of the influence the church could have upon society. A great group of dedicated, faithful, active church members could do more for a nation than all the laws our legislative bodies could enact.

Some time ago I read of a Hollywood actress who claimed to be very religious. She said that she prayed and sought guidance from the Bible. The Hollywood Christian group often meets in her home, but she said she was not a member of any particular church. Do you see what she is doing? She is claiming a kinship with God, she is enjoying all of His blessings, but Christ and the institution He founded are passed by. On the other hand the actor, Gregory Walcott, is a great Christian, a faithful deacon in his church. He said that when he first went to Hollywood he attended the Hollywood Christian group but was not satisfied there. He longed for the fellowship of a local church and was not satisfied until he related himself to a good church in that city.

Thousands of our people have been saved, they have been baptized into the fellowship of some church, then they have moved their place of residence but have never moved their church membership. They soon drift away from God and all things holy. Their lives waste away as far as Christianity is concerned. One woman testified, "The Lord saved me from a rocking chair." And He has saved some people from wasting their lives in worldliness by putting them to work in a church.

Some American soldiers found a ruined church in Germany. In it they found fragments of a statue of Christ. They set about to put all the pieces of the statue together, but they could not locate the hands. When they had finished putting the statue together they put this inscription on the base, "He has no hands but your hands to do His work today." Oh, I beg you to get in the church and go to work for Him.

4. *He calls us to rise up and walk in a life of communion with Christ.* That means prayer and Bible study. This is the secret of power and peace in a Christian's life. Leave these things out and your religion becomes a dead formality. The great preacher, Spurgeon, preached to thousands each Sunday and hundreds were saved. When someone asked him the secret of his power and success, he said, "Look in the basement." And the one who asked him the question found a large group of men praying as Spurgeon preached. And it's as we commune with God that we get power and strength to live the Christian life.

5. *He calls us to rise up and walk as consecrated Christians.* You can get to heaven by trusting Christ as your Saviour, but who wants to get there just by the skin of the teeth? Who wants to get just inside the gate and have no fruit for Jesus, no trophy to lay at His feet? However, it is going to be that way with so many people because they are giving their lives away to the world.

A woman by the name of Sadie Smithson lived in Virginia. She was an ordinary seamstress, but her life was filled with a great disappointment, for she found that she was not acceptable to the society leaders of the town. Her great ambition was to belong to the Laurel Literary Society, but her father was poor, she had to wear cheap clothes, so she was not invited to join. Then she hit upon a plan to win over the society leaders. No one in her town had ever been to Europe. She reasoned that if she went to Europe and came home telling of her experiences, she would be invited to join the Laurel Literary Society. So she scrimped and saved until she had money enough to go to Europe.

While she was over there the war broke out and she was trapped in Belgium. An army officer offered to drive her to a place where she could catch a train to Paris. On the way they became lost and Sadie soon found herself on the battlefield. As she stepped out of the car she heard a soldier cry out, "Water, for God's sake, water." She rushed to find some water and brought it to the dying soldier. All night long she went from man to man, giving water, binding wounds with bandages made from her skirt, and scribbling messages for men who would never see home and loved ones again. The next morning a medical officer found her and asked, "Who are you and what are you doing here?" She replied, "I am Sadie Smithson from Virginia and I've been holding hell back all night."

Before long she was on a ship, returning to America. When she told her experiences to a fellow passenger, this woman said, "Well, the Laurel Literary Society will surely take you in now, they'll be glad to have you as a member." But Sadie answered, "I have been face to face with war and death and hell and God. I have been born again. Do you think that social prestige matters now? No, nothing matters now but God and love and doing things for others in His name."

Oh, if our people would just get their values straightened out, then they would see that these worldly honors are not the things that count. Christ and a life for Him are the things that count.

> Only one life, 'twill soon be past,
> Only what's done for Christ will last.

6. *He calls us to rise up and walk as faithful stewards.* "The tithe . . . is the Lord's: it is holy unto the Lord" (Lev.

27:30). I did not say it, God said it. We should do what God tells us to do. And, as in every other instance, when God gives a commandment He adds a blessing. So He tells us in Malachi that if we bring our tithes into God's storehouse He will open up the windows of heaven and pour out such a blessing that we'll hardly be able to contain it.

Dr. M. Theron Rankin served as secretary of the Southern Baptist Foreign Mission Board after some years of service as a dedicated foreign missionary. After his death several years ago an employee of the Board found a letter written by his father to the Board three years before Dr. Rankin was born. The letter, dated in 1891, said, "I am sending $6.80 for Foreign Missions. It is a tithe of some money I made recently." This was not a large gift, but God paid him off in a marvelous way. His son who was born three years later became a dedicated Christian, a gospel preacher and an effective foreign missionary. God always pays off.

Some years ago a Chicago man by the name of Tom Kane put an unusual advertisement in newspapers all over the country. He offered a generous prize to anyone who had been a true tither and could say that God had not blessed him in it. He received over 10,000 answers and every letter testified to the blessings received. Not one said that he had lost anything. But why do we have to listen to anyone else? Why not just listen to God as he promises to bless the tither?

Pat Neff served as governor of Texas and president of Baylor University. He said on one occasion, "All my life I have heard preachers tell about laying up treasures in heaven, but they never tell how. I figured it out for myself. The only way to get treasure in heaven is to put it in something that is going there. Houses and lands, stocks and bonds are not going to heaven, only men and women, boys and girls are going. So if you want to lay up treasures in heaven, you must put those treasures into the work of winning souls who are going to heaven."

7. *He calls us to rise up and walk in a life of service.* Albert Schweitzer, after he had been serving as a doctor and missionary in Africa for fifty years, was asked if he had

found happiness in the dark continent. He answered by saying, "I have found a place of service and that's happiness enough for anyone."

Some of our missionaries spent many months in a Chinese concentration camp. Their friends in America prayed for them and in due time they were released and came home on the Gripsholm. When their praying friends met them at the dock the missionaries said, "You prayed us home, now we want you to pray us back." "Why do you ask that?" And they answered, "Because we are happiest when we are on the field serving Christ."

You, too, will find your greatest joy and happiness in serving Christ just where God has placed you. God needs more men like Billy Graham, true, but more than that he needs more Smiths and Browns and you and me to serve Him right where we are.

Dr. Perry Webb tells of a New England widow whom everybody called "Miss Anna." She and her friend, Eliza, lived together. Now Miss Anna had an only son, a commercial fisherman. One day a man came to the door and said, "I'm sorry, Miss Anna, but your son has been drowned." Miss Anna went back into the house, wringing her hands. "Eliza, what am I going to do?" she asked. Eliza said, "Just sit down here and ask the Lord to help you." "Do you think He will help me?" Miss Anna asked. "Oh, yes, He will," Eliza replied. So Miss Anna said, "I'm going to talk to Him and tell Him that if He is going to help me, to please put His hand on my head." Then she began to pray, "Lord," she prayed, "I'm just a poor woman and I'm in a heap of trouble. Won't you help me?" Right then Eliza put her hand on Miss Anna's head. When the prayer was ended Miss Anna said, "Eliza, the Lord did put His hand on my head and it felt just like your hand." "Yes, Anna," Eliza said, "it was my hand. When you were praying God said to me, 'Eliza, Anna is in a heap of trouble. Lay your hand on her head for Me.' And that's what I did."

That's our job, that's our service for Christ, just to lay our hands on a poor lost world for Jesus.

8. *He calls us at the end of the way to rise up and walk through the gates of glory.* Oh, what a day that's going to be! We strive and toil and worry and fret down here. Often our hearts are broken and the tears course down our cheeks. But then all of life's trials will be over. We'll be at home with Jesus and our loved ones in a land where we'll never grow old.

Dr. Len G. Broughton once served as pastor of the Baptist Tabernacle in Atlanta. In his congregation there was a fine young man, a devoted Christian who served as an usher. The time came when this young man lay ill upon his death-bed. Dr. Broughton went to see him, sat down by the bed-side and began to talk to the young man about heaven and the future life. As his pastor talked the young man's eyes filled with tears. Then Dr. Broughton took out his handker-chief and wiped those tears away, first from one eye and then from the other. Then the young man smiled up into his pastor's face and said, "Dr. Broughton, the next time my tears are wiped away, they will be wiped away by the loving hand of my heavenly Father." Oh, what a wonderful pros-pect for the children of God!

So, in view of all that He has in store for us, let us rise up and walk with our hands in His until life's little day is over and we see Him face to face in glory.

9

ETERNAL PROFIT AND LOSS

Mark 8:36

The Bible is full of important questions. The first one is the question that God asked when He came down into the Garden of Eden after Adam and Eve had sinned, "Adam, where art thou?" (Gen. 3:9). This is a question for everyone. Where do you stand? Are you on God's side or the world's side? Are you living for Christ or against Him? Are you headed for heaven or for hell? Where art thou? The second question in the Bible is, "Where is Abel thy brother?" (Gen. 4:9). God asked this question of Cain. I ask you, Are you interested in your brother man? Have you witnessed to him? Have you told him about the saving grace of Jesus? Have you tried to help him in his difficulties?

There is Job's question, "If a man die, shall he live again?" (Job 14:14). Jesus answered that question when He rose from the dead and when He said, "Because I live, ye shall live also" (John 14:19). There is the question asked by the Philippian jailer, "What must I do to be saved?" (Acts 16: 30). Paul answered by telling him to believe on the Lord Jesus Christ and he would find salvation. Oh, I wish that lost men would crowd around us today in conviction and ask that same question. Then there is Pilate's important question, "What shall I do then with Jesus who is called Christ?" (Matt. 27:22). This is a question every man must answer. God gave His Son for your redemption, now He asks, "What are you going to do with Him?" The question at the final judgment will not be, "Where did you live or how much money did you make or how many friends did you have?" The question then will be, "What did you do with Jesus Christ?"

Now we come to this tremendous question in my text, "For what shall it profit a man, if he shall gain the whole world, and lose his own soul?" This is a question of profit and loss, not of dollars and cents, but of the eternal soul, not for this world only, but for all of eternity. You may gain fortune and fame and power, but all of these things will profit you nothing if, in gaining them, you lose your soul which must live forever.

I. No Man Can Gain the Whole World

1. *No man can gain all of its wealth.* John D. Rockefeller was worth one and a half billion dollars. At one time his income was $250,000 per day. He died at the ripe old age of ninety-six. Just suppose he had lived to be twice that old and had made $250,000 per day all of those years. And suppose he could have kept it all. When he was 192 years old he would have been worth about ten billion dollars and that's a small part of the world's wealth.

J. P. Morgan was worth a hundred million dollars. He was a great power on Wall Street. The great financiers said, "We could not get along without Mr. Morgan in financial circles." But when Mr. Morgan died on a vacation trip in Southern France, the financial world kept going without a ripple on the waves. It is said that Henry Ford's income at one time was one-half million per day. That over $20,000 per hour, day and night, $333.00 per minute, $5.50 per second. And yet Mr. Ford never gained all the wealth of the world.

At one time Henry Ford was said to be worth two billion

dollars. How much is two billion dollars? Well, suppose you had lived 3,500 years before Christ and that you then possessed two billion dollars. And suppose you had spent or thrown away or burnt up $1,000 per day for these 5,500 years, did you know that today, after disposing of all that money over all those years, you would still be worth several million dollars? I am simply trying to show you that no man can gain all of the wealth of the world.

2. *No man can gain all of its power.* Julius Caesar tried that, but he met his end when the dagger of Brutus pierced his heart. Alexander had conquered all of the known world by the time he was thirty-two years of age, but there were countries and continents about which he knew nothing. Napoleon at one time was about to bring all of Europe to its knees before him, but he met his defeat at Waterloo and died in exile, a broken and brokenhearted man. In more recent days the Kaiser and Hitler and others have set out to conquer the world and they have failed. No man can gain the whole world, its wealth or its power.

II. Men Would Not Be Satisfied If They Could Gain the Whole World

1. *Money doesn't satisfy.* If man has five dollars he wants ten, if he has five thousand he wants ten thousand, if he has five million he wants ten million. Many multimillionaires are still working, even in old age, to amass more millions, not because they need it but because they are not satisfied with what they have.

I heard a preacher tell this story. He and another man had worked side by side in their youth for a dollar per day. Then their paths separated. The other man went on to be a millionaire, this man became a preacher and remained poor. After twenty-five years they met on a train and talked for hours over old times and the changes that the years had brought. In the course of the conversation the preacher asked the millionaire, "Are you as happy and contented now as you were when we worked together side by side for a dollar a day?" And the millionaire answered sadly, "No, I must confess that I do not now have the peace and contentment I had in those days. The cares and responsibilities and obligations brought on by my wealth far outweigh any happiness I have gotten out of it."

The Bible says that "money faileth." Yes, it fails to bring contentment, it fails to build character, it fails to buy one's way into the gates of glory.

2. *Fame and power do not satisfy.* When Alexander the Great was thirty-two years of age, he sat down and wept because there was no more territory for him to conquer. Fame and power didn't satisfy him.

But some of our more recent leaders have learned the way of true satisfaction and have passed on their thoughts to us. President Warren G. Harding died on a trip to the western part of our country. A few days before he died he was speaking from the back platform of a train, and he said, "The world needs more of the tender love of God. And there has never been a better rule for the conduct of men and nations than Christ's Golden Rule." President Calvin Coolidge, speaking one afternoon at a church dedication service, said, "We will never have real peace until we find it through Christ, the prince of peace."

President Woodrow Wilson, speaking to a group of men in Dallas one Sunday afternoon, said, "Long ago I learned to stake my all on Christ. I would not undertake anything without asking for His guidance and help." And David Lloyd George, prime minister of England, said, "For England and for the world, it is either Christ or chaos." We have not chosen Christ and the world today is in a chaotic condition. These men were telling us that only Christ could satisfy the longings of the human heart.

3. *Pleasure doesn't satisfy.* Solomon tried everything under the sun. He became the richest, the wisest, the most-married man in the world. Yet all that he had did not satisfy him. He said, "Vanity of vanities; all is vanity" (Eccl. 1:2). True happiness and joy are not found in the sensual pleasures of this world. Hundreds of years ago God

and man were separated by the sin of Eden's Garden, and man never finds peace until he comes back into right relationship with God.

III. IF A MAN GAINED EVERYTHING AND LOST HIS SOUL, HE WOULD BE MAKING A BAD BARGAIN

1. *It would be a bad bargain because his soul is his most valuable possession.* Suppose that you had a diamond worth $5,000 and I offered you a ten-cent piece of glass for it. You would make a bad bargain if you accepted such an offer. Suppose that you owned a piece of property worth $100,000 and I offered you a ten-dollar bill for it. You would be foolish to consummate such a deal. But how much more foolish is that man who sells his eternal soul for the trivial baubles and pleasures of this world.

No wonder Christ died for our sins. One human soul is worth ten worlds like this one we live in.

2. *It would be a bad bargain because the loss of the soul is the greatest loss.* A man seventy-two years of age stood one morning on the curb of the street, looking at the smoldering ruins of what had been a very prosperous business. He said to a friend, "I am seventy-two years of age, I have lost all I have accumulated over the years. My wife and I will have to start all over again. At our age that is going to be hard. We have lost all our material possessions." It's a terrible loss when an old couple loses all that they have, but that is not the greatest loss.

A young man of twenty-six languished upon a hospital bed. He said to a friend, "The doctors tell me I'll never walk again, I'll be an invalid for life. You know how active and vigorous I have always been. But now I have lost my health and I'll be helpless as long as I live." It is a terrible loss to lose one's health, but that is not the greatest loss.

Dr. L. R. Scarborough, president of the Southwestern Baptist Theological Seminary, tells of an incident that happened on a train one day on which he was a passenger. Across the aisle from him sat a young woman with two children. The youngest child cried continually and it seemed that the mother could not quiet it. So Dr. Scarborough went over and picked up the baby and walked up and down the aisle until it went to sleep. Then he brought the baby back and gently laid it down on the seat in front of the young mother. She immediately burst out into tears of gratitude and grief and Dr. Scarborough said to her, "You seem to be in trouble. I am a minister, is there any way in which I can help you?"

Then the young woman said, "Did you see that man in the next car with the two officers?" "Do you mean the insane man?" he asked. "Yes," she replied, "that man is my husband. He and the children and I have been very happy together, but now he has lost his mind. They are taking him to the asylum and I would much rather that he be taken to his grave. But he has lost his mind." It is a great loss when one loses his mind but even that is not the greatest loss.

The greatest loss is the loss of the soul. Death will heal all of these other losses. It will not matter at the end of the way about the state of your wealth, your health or your mind. The only thing that will matter then will be the condition of your soul, and that will depend upon what you have done with Jesus Christ. Trust Him as your Saviour and all will be well. Leave Him out of your life and you will be lost throughout a long eternity.

IV. The Offers Made for Your Soul

1. *Satan makes his offer.* He says, "Live your life for me, live in sin and unbelief. I will give you the pleasures of this world and at the end of the way I'll take you to live with me in hell forever." That is all Satan can offer you, a few paltry pleasures, a life without happiness and meaning, a cold grave at the end and an eternity in a hell of suffering. Why would any sensible man accept such an offer as that?

Esau sold his birthright for a hot meal. Christ purchased our birthright to eternal life on Calvary's cross. But men everywhere are selling their birthright for the things of this world. Satan is winning the victory over them.

2. *Christ makes His offer*. He says, "Come unto me, all ye that labour and are heavy laden, and I will give you rest" (Matt. 11:28). He says, "Come now, and let us reason together . . . though your sins be as scarlet, they shall be as white as snow; though they be red like crimson, they shall be as wool" (Isa. 1:18). He says, "Him that cometh to me I will in no wise cast out" (John 6:37).

He offers to forgive your sin, to adopt you into the family of God, to write your name down in the Lamb's Book of Life. He offers to give you peace and comfort and happiness. He offers to be with you when you come down to the dark valley and He offers to take you to an eternal home of everlasting bliss. How can anyone reject such an offer, such a wonderful Saviour?

V. Why You Should Accept the Offer of Jesus

1. *Because He loves you best and will do the best for you*. A certain girl left her home and went down into sin. There came a time when she became tired of her sinful life and longed to go back home. She wrote a letter to her family asking for their forgiveness and for permission to come home. When the letter was read in the family circle the angry father said, "No, I'll not take her back. She trailed our good name in the dirt and I'll have nothing more to do with her." Her brother said about the same thing. But her mother's love was greater than that. She called in her pastor, gave him some money and said to him, "Go and find my daughter. Tell her I love her and forgive her and want her to come home."

If I know anything about Christ and the Gospel, I believe that is Christ's message to every lost sinner. He says, "In spite of your sin and disobedience and unbelief I love you with all of My heart. My arms are open wide to receive you and forgive you and give you the best I have in heaven and earth."

Go with me to the cross of Calvary. Jesus is dying on that cross for you. If you had been the only lost person in the world, He would gladly have died just for you. Are you willing to turn your back upon such love, upon such a sacrifice for you? He loves you and wants to do that which is best for you.

2. *Because you're going to need Him someday.* You're going to need Him in life. The way ahead will not always be smooth. Trouble and sorrow lie in wait for everyone of us. You are going to need the help and strength and comfort that He alone can give.

And you are going to need Him in death. Someone asked a soldier as he prepared to go to the front, "Are you afraid of death?" "No," he answered, "I am not afraid of death." "But what about that which comes after death?" he was asked. "Yes," said the soldier, "I am afraid of that time beyond death." And well might one be afraid of the great beyond if he has no hope in Christ.

In a small town a group of young fellows would gather every Sunday in the drugstore, lock all the doors and spend the day in drinking and gambling. They ridiculed the idea of religion and laughed at the people who passed by on the way to church. Then one of the young men lay sick and dying. One of the others went to see him and the dying man said to him, "Go to the boys and tell them to quit drinking and gambling. Tell them to go to church on Sunday and give their lives to the Lord and live for Him. Tell them if they were where I am and could see what I see as I look into eternity, they would turn from their wicked ways and prepare to meet God."

Yes, you are going to need Christ in life, you are going to need Him in death, you are going to need Him at the great Judgment Bar of God. Come to Him now and He'll be there when you need Him.

3. *Because He is your only hope for the future.* "The Son of man came to seek and to save that which was lost" (Luke 19:10). Without Him you are eternally lost, without Him you have no hope. Recently a prominent physicist said, "I do not believe in God, I do not need Christ. When I die I don't want any preacher reading a Scripture or offer-

ing a prayer over me. You can just cremate my body and fling my ashes to the wind, for that's all there is to it." And when he died there was no funeral service, no prayer, no Bible reading. He was cremated and his ashes thrown away. He was a man who had no hope. You may be a very good person. You may reverence the Bible and believe in prayer and want a Christian burial. But if you don't know Christ, if you have not been born again, you are just as lost and just as much without hope as that physicist.

But, thank God, there is hope in Christ. Acts 4:12 says, "Neither is there salvation in any other; for there is none other name under heaven given among men, whereby we must be saved." There is our hope, there is our only hope. The soul without Jesus is a hopeless soul, the soul with Jesus has a hope that is steadfast and sure and eternal.

Dr. A. J. Gordon was pastor of a church in Boston many years ago. One day he met a little boy out in front of the church. The boy was carrying a rusty bird cage in his hands and several little birds were fluttering around on the bottom of the cage, as if they knew they were going to be destroyed. Dr. Gordon said, "Son, where did you get those birds?" The boy answered, "I trapped them out in the field." "What are you going to do with them," the preacher asked. "I'm going to take them home and play with them and have some fun with them." "What will you do with them when you get through playing with them?" Dr. Gordon asked. "Oh," said the boy, "I guess I'll just feed them to an old cat we have around the house." Then Dr. Gordon asked the boy how much he would take for the birds and the boy answered, "Mister, you don't want these birds. They're just little old field birds and they can't sing very well." Dr. Gordon said, "I'll give you two dollars for the cage and the birds." "All right," said the boy, "it's a deal, but you're making a bad bargain." The exchange was made and the boy went whistling down the street, for he had two dollars in his pocket. Dr. Gordon took the cage out behind his church and opened the door of the cage and the birds flew out and went soaring away into the blue, singing as they went.

The next Sunday Dr. Gordon took the empty bird cage to the pulpit to use it in illustrating his sermon. He told his congregation all about the little boy and what had happened to the birds. Then he said, "That little boy said that the birds could not sing very well, but when I released them from the cage they went singing away into the blue, and it seems that they were singing, 'Redeemed, redeemed, redeemed.'"

Oh, my friends, you and I were like those little birds. Satan had us in the cage of sin and was taking us to hell. Then Jesus went to the cross and paid the price for our release and our redemption. Now when we come to Him in simple faith we, too, can sing, "Redeemed, redeemed, I've been redeemed."

I close by saying that it will profit you nothing but sorrow and suffering if you gain the whole world and lose your soul. But it will profit you everything in this life and the life to come if you will only receive Jesus as your Lord and Saviour. Why not come to Him now?

10

SONGS AND SALVATION AT MIDNIGHT

Acts 16:30, 31

For some reason I have never been in jail. But I want to tell you about two preachers who were placed in jail and how this incident was used of God for the salvation of souls and the founding of a church. Paul and Silas were preaching in Philippi, doing the works of God. Then one day they met a girl who had the spirit of divination. We don't know all that this means, possibly she served as a modern "fortune teller" does. We do know that her works were the works of Satan himself. Now a group of men in the city used this girl, they exploited her talents for financial gain. She did the work and they received the money. You can trace the majority of our modern sins back to the motive behind them and you'll find again that "the love of money is the root of all kinds of evil."

Well, Paul saw the plight of this poor girl and with the power given to him of God, he cast out the evil spirit from her. This stirred up a hornet's nest. The men who used the girl saw that they were going to lose money, so they pounced upon Paul and Silas and brought them to the court, where they were accused of teaching false customs. The magistrates commanded that they be beaten, so many stripes were laid on the poor preachers' backs. Then they were locked up in the stocks in the inner part of the prison.

But God had not forgotten His servants. And you can't keep good men down. In spite of the beating and the prison and the stocks, Paul and Silas were able to sing and pray at midnight. They were in great pain, the blood was drying on their backs, they were securely fastened in the stocks, but there was a song in their hearts, because Christ lived within and they knew that "all things work together for good to them that love God, to them who are the called according to his purpose" (Rom. 8:28).

When God heard the prayers and the songs as they rose up to His throne, He sent a mighty earthquake that shook the prison to its foundations. All the doors were opened and all the prisoners were set free. The jailer, in great distress, rushed out of his living quarters. He thought that he was going to lose these important prisoners and that their loss might mean his death at the hands of the magistrates. He drew out his sword and was about to kill himself, when Paul cried out, "Stop, stop, do thyself no harm. We are all here" (Acts 16:28).

Then the jailer rushed in and cried out to Paul and Silas, "Sirs, what must I do to be saved?" (verse 30). And Paul answered, "Believe on the Lord Jesus Christ, and thou shalt be saved, and thy house" (verse 31). So Paul, always on the alert, preached a gospel sermon to the jailer and all that were in his house. The jailer, who had viciously laid the stripes on the backs of these men the previous evening, now tenderly washed their stripes. Then the jailer and his family were baptized and, after this solemn ceremony, all of them sat down to eat, rejoicing that salvation had come to the jailer's heart and home and family.

Here is a good picture of salvation in simple form. First, these people heard the Gospel and were convicted of their sins. Second, they believed and were saved. Third, they gave evidence of their conversion by washing the stripes of Paul and Silas. Fourth, they were baptized in obedience to the righteous command of the Lord Jesus Christ. Fifth, they sat down at the table and enjoyed a meal. In like manner the Christian sits at the Lord's table and enjoys the good things of heaven and earth.

Now we know that there are two conditions of salvation, "repentance toward God, and faith toward our Lord Jesus Christ" (Acts 20:21). All through the Bible repentance comes before faith. Repentance is a change of mind and heart toward God. Why, then, did Paul tell the jailer simply to "believe on the Lord Jesus Christ"? Surely he knew that already the jailer was in a penitent frame of mind, he was already repenting of his sin. When he asked, "What must I do to be saved?" he was simply saying, "I've had a change of heart, I'm willing to do anything you say." So, in effect Paul was saying, "You've repented of your sin, now place your faith in the Lord Jesus Christ and you'll be saved."

I. The Jailer's Question

He asked the question that every man should ask, "What must I do to be saved?" He did not ask how to get a better job, he did not ask how to raise his family, he did not ask how to get an education, he did not ask how to make money, he did not ask how to get along with his neighbors. No, he asked the most important question a man can ask, "What must I do to be saved?" When a man asks that question he is facing up to God. When a man asks that question, he is thinking in eternal terms. When a man asks that question he is asking the most important question he will ever ask. Oh, that more men would ask that question of us today.

This question tells us that the man knew he was lost. What does it mean to be lost? It means to be cut off from God for this world and the next. It means that sin stands between you and a holy God. It means that one day you'll die and go out to live in a hell of endless, conscious suffering.

What made the jailer realize that he was lost? It may have been the Christlike attitude exhibited by the preachers when he beat them. It may have been the songs and prayers he heard at midnight. It may have been the fear brought on by the earthquake. The Holy Spirit used all these things to show him the difference between himself and these preachers and how he needed the thing that they had.

There are only two classes of people in the world, the saved and the lost. Whether they are rich or poor, learned or ignorant, great or small, they are either saved or lost. "He that believeth on the Son hath everlasting life: and he that believeth not the Son shall not see life; but the wrath of God abideth on him" (John 3:36). The jailer believed that he belonged to this "lost" group. No one is ever saved until he realizes that he is lost.

General O. O. Howard was stationed at a Florida camp. One night he went to a church service. The pastor preached and gave an invitation and several men went forward to accept Christ. Just behind General Howard two officers were mocking and ridiculing what had happened. In order to show that he did not approve of their attitude the general also went forward. The pastor knelt by the general, talked to him about Christ and prayed for him. The general went back to his quarters and began to read his Bible. Soon he was on his knees, giving his heart to Jesus. He soon arose, shouting, "Glory to God, salvation in Christ is wonderful." He began to pray for all the men in the camp to be saved. Before they left Florida all but one of his men had been saved. Three years later he met that man on a Virginia battlefield. He said to the general, "Down in Florida you got something that I need and wish I had." In a few minutes the general had led the man to Christ and two weeks later the man was killed on the field of battle.

That's what a man needs to realize, that he lacks something, that he is lost without Christ. Life is never complete outside of Christ. Men need Him to give help and hope in this world and heaven at the end of the way.

The jailer's question revealed that he wanted to be saved. A man is never saved until he desires salvation. God never saves a man against his will. The jailer knew that the preachers had something that he didn't have. He knew that if they could sing at midnight, with the blood drying on their backs, they had something that only Christ could give.

The jailer's question showed that he did not know how to be saved. There was some excuse for him, but there is no excuse for men today. The jailer didn't have an open Bible as you do today, he didn't get to hear the Gospel as you do, he didn't have a preacher before this time to explain to him the way of life. There is no excuse for you. You have every aid to salvation today. If you die and go to hell, you'll have to climb over the church, over the sermons you have heard, over the call of the Holy Spirit, over the prayers of loved ones, and a thousand other things.

A man doesn't have to know all the Bible to be saved. He needs only to know that he is a sinner and that Christ can save Him. In a certain meeting a man said to the preacher, "I'll accept Christ if you answer a question for me. Where did Cain get his wife?" The preacher knew that the man was quibbling, so he said, "Young man, what is your sin?" The man left the church. Two weeks later he ran away with another man's wife. It wasn't Cain's wife that bothered him, but another man's wife. You ask questions and give excuses for not being a Christian. If you will give up your sin and trust Christ, He will fill your heart with joy, settle all your questions and give you the peace that passes all understanding.

We note that the jailer came in great humility. He fell on his knees and said, "What must I do to be saved?" If you expect to be saved, you must come humbly. Jesus said, "Except ye . . . become as little children ye shall not enter into the kingdom of heaven" (Matt. 18:3). To be saved you must come humbly to Christ, not boasting of your own goodness, but acknowledging your pitiful need of Him.

> Nothing in my hand I bring,
> Simply to Thy cross I cling.

II. Paul's Answer

When the jailer cried out, "What must I do to be saved?"

Paul answered, "Believe on the Lord Jesus Christ, and thou shalt be saved." Paul didn't say, "That's all in the hands of God, if He wants you to be saved He'll save you." Yet some people do believe this. They go through life expecting God to do some fantastic thing to save them, when He has already done everything necessary to save anyone who will come to Him through faith in the Lord Jesus Christ. So it's your move, God has made the sacrifice necessary to save you, now He offers you salvation as a free gift. It is simply up to you to accept the gift. You do that by opening up your heart and receiving Jesus Christ as your Saviour.

Paul did not say to the jailer, "Turn over a new leaf, live a good life and you'll be saved." When the New Year comes around a man often examines himself and resolves to live a better life. That doesn't mean that he has met Christ and been saved. Here is a man who is a habitual drinker. The doctor tells him that his drinking will ruin his health, so he gives up liquor. That doesn't mean that he has had an encounter with Christ.

Nicodemus was a good moral man, he had to be to become a member of the Sanhedrin. But Jesus told him that he had to be born again. He meant that Nicodemus needed a new heart and a new life. Just lopping off some sins and bad habits doesn't bring salvation. However, when Christ does come into the heart these things go out. "If any man be in Christ, he is a new creature: old things are passed away; behold, all things are become new" (II Cor. 5:17).

Paul didn't tell the jailer that he could be saved by treating his fellow man rightly. I was called upon to conduct a funeral and a member of the dead man's family said to me, "He wasn't a Christian, he never joined a church. But he never harmed anybody, he never said anything against anybody, he treated everybody rightly." And this person thought that the man had gone to heaven because of that. But that is not enough. Salvation is based upon the way you treat Christ, not the way you treat your fellow man. If you get right with Christ you will surely treat others in the right way, but just being a good friend or a good neighbor does not save anyone.

Paul didn't tell the jailer that he could be saved by simply joining a church. However, I believe that if a man has had the tremendous experience of conversion to Christ, he will want to join a church and nothing will keep him out. But simply getting your name on a church roll without a previous experience with Christ is an empty performance. I like to see a church grow, I like to see new members being added. But we must insist always on a regenerated church membership. Men must first be saved, then they are ready to join a church. That is the New Testament way.

I am often asked the question, "Are Catholics saved? The church is supreme to them, are they saved?" The same thing applies to them as to Baptists, Methodists, Presbyterians and all others. If they have repented of their sin and put their faith in Christ, they are saved. If all they have done is to join the church, any church, they are still lost. Now every Christian ought to be a church member. They ought to belong to a church where they live. If you say you can live as well outside the church as you can inside, you are saying that Christ was wrong when He founded the church and left it on the earth.

Paul did not tell the jailer that baptism could save him. But you would be surprised to learn how many churches teach that baptism is the door into the kingdom of God. I went into a Catholic hospital to see a man who was critically ill. As I came out of his room a nun asked me about his condition. I told her that I was afraid that he was dying, that he was not a Christian. "Do you mean to tell me he hasn't been baptized?" she asked me. I said, "He isn't a Christian and he hasn't been baptized." She literally ran to get the Catholic chaplain to come and pour a little water on the man's head, as if that would insure his entrance into the kingdom of heaven.

I read about a prominent man who was dying. He was unconscious. A preacher was called in and the man was propped up on the pillows. The preacher poured some water on the man's head and said, "I baptize thee in the name of the Father and of the Son and of the Holy Spirit." Now what did that have to do with salvation, how many sins were washed away? Baptism is an outward thing, salvation is an inner thing. The idea of salvation through baptism came from the dark ages. The religious teachers said that an unbaptized person would go to hell, so they were baptized to get to heaven. But let us get back to Paul's answer, "Believe on the Lord Jesus Christ, and thou shalt be saved."

Now we must not minimize the importance of baptism and the Lord's Supper. They should be given their rightful place. Both ordinances are to be observed after salvation as a matter of obedience. Baptism of the believer is a one-time thing, the Lord's Supper is to be observed often "in remembrance" of Jesus. But salvation must come before either of these ordinances. Jesus Christ can save the deepest-dyed sinner in the world without the help of water or the bread and the wine of the Lord's Supper.

Paul did not tell the jailer that he would be saved if he lived a good life. We ought to live at our best always, but you can be the best moral man in the world and still go to hell. Your goodness can never save you, your faith in the crucified Son of God is the thing that saves you. Here is a man who is kind, helpful, clean and considerate. But he is not a Christian. Is he really and truly a good man? I say that he is not. Although Christ loved him and died for him, that man is saying, "Get out of the way, Christ, I don't need you. I can get along all right without you." Is he a good man? No, I say he has committed the blackest sin this side of hell.

Dr. L. R. Scarborough preached on the doctrine of repentance in a certain revival. A fine young woman came up and said to him, "I do not need to repent. I have been brought up in a fine home. I have gone to Sunday school and church all of my life. I have always lived a good life, I don't need to repent." Dr. Scarborough then asked her, "Have you accepted God's Son who died for you?" She answered, "No." "Then," said the preacher, "you might as well be the meanest person this side of hell. You are lost because you have rejected Christ." Later she came to the front weeping and saying, "I am not worthy of Christ, but tell me how to be saved."

Paul did not tell the jailer to give some money in order to be saved. We ought to give as a matter of love for Christ, but giving will not save you. I knew of a man who would send generous checks to the church, but he wouldn't turn to Christ because he was holding on to an immoral sin in his life. You may give millions to the cause of Christ, but you'll never be saved until you turn from your sin and turn in faith to Jesus.

Now don't get me wrong. Men ought to live good clean lives, they ought to treat people rightly, they ought to be baptized, they ought to be faithful church members, they ought to give their money. But all of these things will not save you. It takes God's grace and your faith to bring about salvation. All of these good works done before salvation will gain you no merit with God. But these good works done after you are saved will bring you a reward in heaven.

A little girl was born into a Montana rancher's home. A neighbor gave her a Newfoundland puppy and the little girl and the dog grew up as inseparable companions. When the girl was five years old the dog had become a giant in size. One day the girl's father went to town and left the gate open. The little girl slipped away and the dog went with her. She was not missed for more than an hour. When the father came home and found her missing, he was beside himself. A frantic search was begun, but it was several hours before they found the little girl in the mountains, far from home. Her dress was torn, her face was covered with dust and tears. She was asleep and her faithful dog was guarding her. Her father saw blood on the dog and knew there had been a fight. He looked over in the bushes and found two dead wolves. He knew then that the dog had killed them when they attacked the little girl. The dog had been seriously wounded. The man took the girl and the dog home. The girl was not harmed, but the dog died the next day. The man and his wife wept over his death, they made a coffin for him and buried him. Then they placed a stone over his head which read, "Oh, how we loved him."

Will a man and woman love a dog who saved their daughter's life and will you not love a Saviour who died for you enough to confess Him as your Saviour and to follow Him in baptism and a good Christian life? Oh, if you have been saved you will do these things as a proof of your salvation.

Paul simply told the jailer to "believe on the Lord Jesus Christ." This means more than a mere mental opinion about Jesus. You can believe all that the Bible says about Him and be forever lost. To "believe on" Christ means to trust Him with all of your heart, mind and soul for time and eternity. It means that you come to lean on Him for salvation like your body rests on that church pew. It means, "Here, Lord, I give myself to Thee, 'tis all that I can do."

Now Paul knew what he was talking about. He was an educated man, he had completed his studies in Tarsus and had taken post-graduate work under Gamaliel. But the greatest thing about him was that he knew Jesus Christ and the way of salvation. Years before this time he had had a great experience of salvation when he met Jesus on the Damascus Road and he could never get away from that experience. He had been walking with Jesus ever since that time. Now he could say with absolute assurance, "I know whom I have believed, and am persuaded that he is able to keep that which I have committed unto him against that day" (II Tim. 1:12). He could say, "I was the chief of sinners. He saved me and I know He can save you."

Paul did not say, "Believe now and maybe at the end of the way He will save you." Salvation is a present-tense thing. If you are not saved in life, you won't be saved in death. Paul meant that the jailer would be saved the minute he trusted in Christ.

When I went to the big city as a boy I lived for a time in the home of a friend. They had something in their bathroom that I had never seen. It was an "instantaneous heater." You would light the gas heater and minutes later when you turned on the water, it would be hot. Salvation is more instantaneous than that. The minute you believe, you are saved. You become a child of God and your name is written in the Lamb's Book of Life.

Now when Paul told the jailer how to be saved, the jailer didn't say, "I'll think about it, I'll wait a while, I'll trust Him someday." He believed on Jesus that night and he was saved that night. I am asking you to trust Him now. Do not wait. Tomorrow may be too late, there is danger in delay, there is peril in postponement. Come now as the Holy Spirit pleads with you to come.

A rabbi once said to his students, "You should repent the day before you die." "But we don't know when we're going to die," they replied. "Then," said the wise rabbi, "you should repent today."

The longer you put off your decision for Christ, the harder it becomes to make that decision. Christmas Evans uses the example of a blacksmith's dog for an illustration of this truth. When the dog first came to the shop it would become frightened when the sparks fell from the anvil. But after a time the dog had become so accustomed to the flying sparks that he would go to sleep under the anvil, with the sparks falling all around him. And so men hear the Gospel and are moved and stirred and convicted, but they go on without Christ. Soon they are so hardened to the call of Christ that nothing moves them.

Paul evidently started a church at Philippi. I am sure the jailer must have been a charter member and probably one of the deacons because anyone with such a glorious experience of salvation will want to have fellowship with other Christians in worship and service. I imagine that he often gathered a group around him and said, "Let me tell you what happened the night of the earthquake."

Someday in heaven I am going to ask Jesus to tell me where the jailer's mansion is located. When I find him I am going to say, "Tell me about the night of the earthquake." Then he will tell me the story as it is recorded in the Book of Acts. Then as we look out the window he will say, "There's Jesus now. Oh, how I love Him for saving my soul." Dear lost soul, He wants to save you.

General Robert E. Lee reported the death of one of his young officers. He was a fine Christian and greatly admired by all of the men. His body was taken home to Alabama. As the casket was rolled in the front door, his mother stood there, the tears streaming down her face. But she was singing, "Washed in the blood of the Lamb."

Don't you want it to be that way when you die? "Believe on the Lord Jesus Christ, and thou shalt be saved."

11

THE GREATEST THING THAT COULD HAPPEN
TO THE WORLD

John 14:1-3

What is the greatest thing that could happen to the world? Someone will say, "Oh, if we could only have world peace, that would be the best thing that could happen to the world. Then our finest men would not be giving their lives away on the bloody battlefields of the world, then we could take the billions that we spend on war and defense for the benefit of mankind." Yes, that would be a wonderful thing.

Someone else would say, "Oh, if we could only supply the physical needs of men all over the world, that would be great. Millions live in poverty, millions go to bed hungry every night. If we could supply them with good houses and good clothes and good food, that would be wonderful." Yes, that would be wonderful.

Someone else will say, "Oh, if we could only find a cure for cancer and the many other diseases that cut people down, that would be great." Indeed it would be wonderful for every day we hear of many fine people who are succumbing to these diseases. Someone else would say, "Oh, if we could just settle the race question and get rid of communism and let all men live together as brothers, that would be wonderful." Indeed it would be.

But the greatest thing that could happen to the world would be for Christ to return. He would solve all of our problems, He would straighten out the world, He would give us an era of peace, plenty and prosperity. Now as I speak of His coming, I want to use four points.

I. THE PROOF OF HIS COMING
II. THE PLAN OF HIS COMING
III. THE PURPOSE OF HIS COMING
IV. THE PREPARATION FOR HIS COMING

I. THE PROOF OF HIS COMING

That proof is found in one Book, the infallible Book, the Bible, the Word of God. The Bible is God's Word to man. If you believe in the Bible you must believe that Jesus is coming again.

The Old Testament is full of this truth. In the Old Testament there are two lines of prophecy concerning Christ's coming to the world. The first line tells us of His first coming as a Suffering Saviour. In Isaiah 53, we read that "He was wounded for our transgressions, he was bruised for our iniquities: the chastisement of our peace was upon him; and with his stripes we are healed" (verse 5). There are many other passages in the Old Testament which give us pictures similar to this one.

Now as you read such Scripture passages, what do you see? You see Him in Gethsemane, sweating great drops of blood. You see Jesus Christ giving His back to the smiters, you see the bloody welts forming, you see the blood flowing down to His lower garments. You see Him on Calvary, bleeding His life away for us and enduring the most excruciating pain. All this is a fulfillment of the first line of prophecy in the Old Testament.

The second line of prophecy in the Old Testament concerns His coming in glory as King of kings and Lord of lords. As we read these prophecies we see a mighty Conqueror coming in great majesty and power. This is exactly opposite to the picture of His coming as a Suffering Servant. The first line of prophecy portrays His first coming, when He suffered and died for our sins. The second line of prophecy portrays Him coming as the great God of heaven and earth.

Now in John 1:11 we read that "He came unto his own,

and his own received him not." Why didn't His people receive Him? Over the centuries they had looked forward to the coming of the Messiah, they had talked about it, sung about it, longed for it, prayed for it. Why didn't they receive Him when He did come? It was because they were looking at only one line of prophecy. They expected Him to come as a conquering King who would throw off the yoke of Rome and set up again the kingdom of Israel in all the glory that was theirs during the Golden Age of King David. They neglected the first line of prophecy, even as many people today neglect the second line. So when He came to suffer and die as the poorest of the poor and the humblest of the humble, they did not recognize Him and did not receive Him.

But today we stand on this side of Calvary, and as we study Bible prophecy we are looking for Him to come as Lord of lords and King of kings. We are not looking for a humble peasant to come and die on the cross, we are looking for "the glorious appearing of the great God and our Saviour Jesus Christ" (Tit. 2:13).

If you want positive proof of His coming, just read the New Testament and this great truth will leap out at you from nearly every page. It is mentioned 318 times in the New Testament. One out of every twenty-five verses refers to it. Yet even some modern preachers cannot see it. A young fellow who was a member of the church where I was pastor had a flat tire just outside of a large church. The pastor of that church came out and engaged the young man in conversation. This young man had heard me preach on the Second Coming and told the big preacher what he believed about it and what the Bible said about it. The preacher positively "hooted" at the idea and said, "You don't expect me to believe that stuff, do you?"

Now this attitude proved two things. First, that preacher did not believe the Bible. Second, prophecy was still being fulfilled, for God said that in the latter days scoffers would arise who would mock the idea of the Lord's return. Do you believe the Bible? Then you must believe in the Saviour's return. The proof of His coming is in the Bible.

II. The Plan of His Coming

There are really two phases of His coming, in fact, two separate comings. Twice the Lord Himself will break through the blue, leave heaven and come back.

1. *First, Jesus will come in the air.* At that time He will not touch the world, but will come in the air for a special purpose. Listen to the plain truth in I Thess. 4:13-18, "But I would not have you to be ignorant, brethren, concerning them which are asleep, that ye sorrow not, even as others which have no hope. For if we believe that Jesus died and rose again, even so them also which sleep in Jesus will God bring with him. For this we say unto you by the word of the Lord, that we which are alive and remain unto the coming of the Lord shall not precede them which are asleep. For the Lord himself shall descend from heaven with a shout, with the voice of the archangel, and with the trump of God: and the dead in Christ shall rise first: Then we which are alive and remain shall be caught up together with them in the clouds; to meet the Lord in the air: and so shall we ever be with the Lord. Wherefore comfort one another with these words."

Can any words be plainer than these? It is not hard to understand that Jesus is coming in the air for His own. The Holy Spirit here emphasizes the fact that it is the Lord Himself and not another who is coming. You see, some of the Thessalonian Christians had died and their loved ones, who were looking for Jesus to come back, were concerned that their departed loved ones would not be present to share the joys that would come when Jesus returned. So Paul said, "I don't want you to worry. When Jesus comes they will be with Him and we'll all be together and with the Lord forever."

So we see that He will come first in the air and those who love and trust Him will go up to meet Him, both the dead and the living saints. Now that's the event that we are looking forward to. There were many prophecies that had to be fulfilled between the time that He went up in a cloud and the time that He will return in the air. Did you know that every one of these prophecies has now been fulfilled. So He could come at any minute. Any minute we could hear the shout, the voice of the archangel and the trumpet of the Lord.

A preacher said to a group of people, "Do you think Jesus will come back today?" They replied, "We think not." And he quoted the Scripture to them, "In such an hour as ye think not the Son of man cometh" (Matt. 24:44).

As I think of the conditions of the world today I am led to believe that His coming must be near. We think of wars and bloodshed and violence all over the world. We think of sin and graft and riots and arson and looting and all the other evils right here in our own country. Who can straighten it all out? The president can't do it, Congress can't do it, the United Nations can't do it. It will take more than a Superman to do it, it will take a Supernatural Man to do it. And that Man is the Lord Jesus Christ. He is the only One who can straighten out the world. So as I look at the conditions of the world, I don't see how things can go on as they are much longer. He will have to come back to straighten out the world.

2. *Then Jesus will come back to this world.* First, He comes in the air to take up all Christians, dead and living, into heaven. At the Judgment Seat He will judge every Christian's works and issue them their rewards. During this time the Tribulation Period will take place on earth, a period of approximately seven years. As the name implies, it will be a time of great trouble and distress, but Christians will not be here, they'll be gone up to be with the Lord. This time He will not stop in the air, but will come down to earth and His feet shall stand on the Mount of Olives. He will not be alone; He will be followed by all of His people of all ages.

So let us think clearly of the plan of His coming. He will come first in the air for His saints. After a period in heaven, He will come to earth with His saints.

III. THE PURPOSE OF HIS COMING

1. *Why will He come in the air?* First, He will come to raise up all the Christian dead, from their graves, from the bottom of the sea, from the sands of the desert. Paul said, "The dead in Christ shall rise first." As soon as He comes in the air and gives a shout, every dead Christian will rise up to meet Him. His favorite word is the word, "Come." Maybe that is what He will shout when He comes in the air. And as those bodies rise up to meet Him they will not be as they were when they died. No, those broken, diseased, emaciated, aged bodies will be transformed into His own glorious likeness (Phil. 3:21). He performed many marvelous miracles when He was here on earth, but when He changes us who are sorry sinful human beings into His own glorious likeness, when He makes us like Himself, that will be the greatest miracle of all.

When a Christian dies his body is buried in the ground, but his soul, his spirit, his real self, goes up to be with the Lord. Paul said, "Absent from the body, present with the Lord" (II Cor. 5:8). He said, "I am in a strait betwixt two, having a desire to depart, and be with Christ; which is far better" (Phil. 1:23). He was simply bearing out this truth, that the soul and body are separated at death, with the soul going on to be with Jesus. Then when Jesus comes in the air He will bring our spirits, our souls, with Him. He will raise up our bodies, soul and body will be joined again and then, and not until then, will our salvation be complete.

Next, when He comes in the air He will catch up all living Christians to be with Him. They will not go through the experience of death. Some may be in the church, some may be at home, some may be at work, some may be asleep. But, wherever they may be, they'll be snatched up from the world like an eagle snatches up its prey and carries it to the heights. Not one will be left. All of them will go up to meet the Lord and their loved ones in the air. And as they go up they, too, will be transformed into His glorious likeness.

You see, the tribulation period is coming to this world. All the wars and bloodshed and troubles and accidents and tornadoes and sorrows of this present age will not compare with that period. God doesn't want His people to suffer these things, so He takes them up to be with Him. That is why He will come in the air.

2. *Why will He come later to the earth in glory?* When He came the first time He was born in a stable and laid in a manger. He lived as a poor man all the days of His life. He said that He had no place to lay His head. He was cursed and maligned and humiliated. He was beaten and buffeted and spat upon. He was crowned with thorns. He was crucified between two thieves. Oh, what awful treatment for the King of heaven. Now all of this must be changed, so we see Him coming this time in glory. All the saints and angels of heaven will be with Him. He will come bedecked with many crowns, He will arrive in splendor and majesty such as no king ever knew.

What will happen when He gets here? In my book, *Seven Simple Sermons on the Second Coming*, I have an entire chapter on this subject, but in this message I can give you only a bare outline.

The battle of Armageddon will take place, the greatest battle the world has ever known. In this battle Jesus will slay all the armies gathered against Him and His people. Then He will cast the Antichrist and the false prophet, who caused all the trouble in the tribulation period, into the lake of fire. He will then judge the nations according to their treatment of His brethren. Satan will then be chained and bound for a thousand years. The millennium is to be a great period of peace on earth, so Satan must be put away, since he is the father of all trouble and sin.

The millennium will then begin, a thousand years of peace, plenty and prosperity, with Jesus reigning over all as the Prince of Peace. When the thousand years are over Satan will be loosed for a season, then he, too, will be cast into the lake of fire to "be tormented day and night for ever and ever" (Rev. 20:10). Then Christ will set up the Great White Throne Judgment, raise up all the lost people, judge them and cast them into the lake of fire (Rev. 20:15). Then the eternal ages will begin, with Christ and all His people in heaven and Satan and all of his people in hell.

Now let us review a minute. Christ will come in the air and take all Christians, living or dead, up to be with Him. Then He will come to earth with His saints, all Christians. He will take over the world and reign for a thousand years. After all the events connected with and following this period, all Christians will be in heaven with Jesus and all the lost will be in hell with Satan. Then the eternal ages will begin.

IV. The Preparation for His Coming

1. *We prepare by coming to Him for salvation.* There is only one way to be saved and that is through "repentance toward God, and faith toward our Lord Jesus Christ" (Acts 20:21). When Jesus comes in the air, when the trumpet sounds, there'll be no more opportunities for you to be saved.

When Paul came to the end of the way, he said, "I am now ready to be offered, and the time of my departure is at hand. I have fought a good fight, I have finished my course, I have kept the faith: Henceforth there is laid up for me a crown of righteousness, which the Lord, the righteous judge, shall give me at that day: and not to me only, but unto all them also that love his appearing" (II Tim. 4:6-8). How was Paul able to say this? Was it because He had worked so hard for Christ? Was it because he had won so many souls and established so many churches? Was it because he always preached the true Gospel? Was it because he suffered so many things for Jesus? No, these things do not save. He was ready and anticipating a crown because one day he had met Christ on the Damascus road and had put all of his faith in Him? Are you ready to meet Jesus in the air? Not until you have met Him here on earth.

I was conducting a revival in the church where I was pastor. One of my deacons came up to me and said, "My wife's niece, who lives with us, is under deep conviction. Can you come out and talk to her after church tonight?" I agreed to go, along with my wife. We sat down in the living room and talked to the young woman about her relationship to God. Then I noticed a broad stripe running across the rug. I asked my wife and the deacon and his wife to come over with me on one side of the stripe. This left the young lady standing alone on the other side of the stripe. Then I explained to her that if she rejected Christ, she would be on the hell side of eternity and we who had accepted Him would be on the heaven side. Then I urged her to cross over the stripe and get on our side, Christ's side, the heaven side. She didn't walk, she ran across the stripe and said, "I'll trust Christ as my Saviour right now."

Now I had Scripture to back me up in my proposition, for the Bible says that in eternity there is a great gulf fixed between heaven and hell, between the home of the saved and the home of the lost. And we decide in this world the side of the gulf we want to be on in eternity. Our destinies are fixed here. Out there, there can be no crossing over the gulf from one place to the other.

During World War II a doctor in a hospital ward heard a soldier saying, "The blood, oh, the blood." He thought the boy was upset by the sight of so much blood on the battlefield and in the hospital, so he tried to divert the boy's attention. But the soldier said, "I'm not thinking about the blood of the battlefield, I was just thinking of how precious is the blood of Christ when one is dying, as I am." That boy had the right kind of faith.

2. *We prepare by living consecrated Christian lives.* The Bible says that if a man has this hope, he purifies himself. If we know we may meet Him at any minute, we should clean up our lives and throw aside everything that would be wrong in His sight.

A little girl heard her mother and a neighbor talking about the return of the Lord. Later the little girl's mother went upstairs and found her looking out of the window. She asked the girl what she was doing, and she replied, "I heard you and our neighbor saying that Jesus might come back at any minute. So I came upstairs, took a bath, put on my best dress, and now I am looking for Him." Oh, some of us need to take a spiritual bath. We need to throw off the old clothes of sin and worldliness and put on the new garments of consecrated Christian living.

3. *We prepare by giving Him our best service.* Before He went away He said, "Occupy until I come and I'll bring your reward with me." I am afraid some Christians will have no reward. They have been saved, but they give no service to the Lord. They'll get to heaven, but their works will be burned up. They say, "Someday I'm going to serve God, someday I'll witness for Him, someday I'll tithe." But "someday" never comes. If Jesus returned today you would curse yourself for not serving Him better.

4. *We prepare by loving His appearing.* Some people say, "I believe in His coming, but I don't want Him to come soon." They don't love His appearing. But if they knew all the glorious things that would happen to them if He came back today, they would say with dear old John on the Isle of Patmos, "Even so, come, Lord Jesus" (Rev. 22:20). That would not only be the greatest thing that could happen to the world, it would be the greatest thing that could happen to us all.

During World War II many of our finest young men went overseas. I saw their pictures in the homes of my people, their service stars in the window. Their loved ones longed for the time when the war would be over and the men would be coming home. Then we heard that the war was coming to a close. A mother would phone me and say, "My son is coming." A wife would say, "Pastor, my husband is safe and he's coming home." A girl would say, "My sweetheart is coming home and we're going to be married." Oh, how they longed for the coming of their loved ones and how sweet and wonderful it was when they returned. That's the way we ought to feel about the coming of Jesus. We should love His appearing, and when He does come, how marvelous it will be.

So I invite you to Jesus right now. Can't you see Him as He hangs on the cross? The crown of thorns is piercing His brow. The great nails have pierced His hands and feet. The spear will be thrust into His side. He bore all the sufferings of hell as He hung there on the cross. And it was all for you and me. Today He comes to you with outstretched hands. He says, "I've come to wash away your sins, to fill your heart with peace and joy, to be your Best Friend, to walk down every pathway with you and at last to lead you on to the streets of glory." How can you turn down such a Saviour?

Two young men left their homes and soon went down into deepest sin. In a card game one night there was a quarrel and one of them was shot. His comrade managed to get him out of the room and placed him under a tree. He rolled up his coat and made a pillow for the dying boy. The boy who had been shot said, "Buddy, I can't die like this. Maybe God will be merciful if you ask Him to forgive me. I am in such pain that I can't pray. Won't you pray for me?" The other boy said, "I can't pray, but I am trying to think of some Bible verses I learned in Sunday school. One of them said that God loved us enough to give His Son for us and that if we trusted Him we would have everlasting life. Another verse said that if we came to Him He would in no wise cast us out."

The dying boy said, "Those are precious words. I'll do that, I'll trust Jesus right now and ask Him to forgive me and save me." He closed His eyes for a minute, then he said, "Can you sing a song for me?" And his buddy began to croon, "Rock of ages, cleft for me, Let me hide myself in Thee; Let the water and the blood, from Thy wounded side which flowed, Be of sin the double cure, Save from wrath and make me pure." When he finished the song, the dying boy had his hand lifted up toward heaven and he said, "Buddy, I've got hold of the hand of Jesus and I'll never let it go." And soon he was gone.

Oh, friend, the hand of Christ is reaching down to you right now. Take hold of that hand, put all of your faith and trust in Christ. Then when He comes back you'll be ready. You won't be afraid and you won't be ashamed.